HIGHER FINANCE

How to Live Debt-Free

by

Frederick K.C. Price, D.D.

FAITH ONE
PUBLISHING

LOS ANGELES, CALIFORNIA

Unless otherwise indicated, all Scripture quotations are taken from the *New King James Version* of the Bible. Copyright 1979, 1980, 1982 Thomas Nelson, Inc. Publishers. Used by permission.

3rd Printing

HIGHER FINANCE
How to Live Debt-Free
ISBN 1-883798-41-8
Copyright © 1999 by
Frederick K.C. Price, D.D.
PO Box 90000
Los Angeles, CA 90009

Published by Faith One Publishing
7901 South Vermont Avenue
Los Angeles, California 90044

Printed in the United States of America. All rights reserved under International Copyright Law. Contents and/or cover may not be reproduced in whole or in part, in any form or by any means, without the express written consent of the Publisher.

TABLE OF CONTENTS

INTRODUCTION

Christians as a whole lack knowledge of their rights and privileges. The tragedy of it all is that the level of ignorance has been perpetuated from pulpits across the world. Christians are being nourished and nurtured on the idea that poverty is a badge of honor. There is a disdain for prosperity that borders on arrogance, even in those thought to be educated in God's Word.

The bottom line is that Satan's people are rolling in riches while the children of God go beggingly along in sheer ignorance, coupled with a whole lot of disobedience. If God's people would study His Word for themselves, they would know they are not honoring Him with their poverty.

On the other hand, Satan is happy that so many Believers are ignorant, because it helps the world system to remain intact. Poverty is built into that system. For most, there is no way to crawl out of the depths of poverty, unless they do it God's way. Those who have relied on government handouts would do well to read and heed God's Word regarding tithes and offerings, because the government systems are changing rapidly.

God has the only 100 percent workable financial plan, the only plan to deliver you out of the grips of lack, want and poverty, and into the prosperity that Christ shed His blood for us to have.

INTRODUCTION

Tithes and offerings are His way.

In this book, you will be presented a wide range of Scriptures — from both the Old and New Testaments — that prove to you that God wants you to prosper.

And as you read the financial commands in this book and match them with God's Word, you will gain greater insight into what tithing is all about. I believe you will once and for all be armed with enough information to shed the notion that your offerings and tithes are "only for the preacher." You will finally understand that God initiated the tithe for *your* benefit. And therse is great joy as well as many rewards and blessings yet to be discovered as you become a willing and obedient tither.

ONE

GOD HAS A FINANCIAL PLAN

I never tire of hearing about the tithe because it has been such a tremendous blessing for me. Tithing has placed me in a position where I can be a giver.

I spent most of my life grubbing, trying to make ends meet. It was always a struggle just to have enough for myself. How can you give to others unless you are first able to take care of yourself and your own family?

For years, I could not tithe because I could not afford to. I did not have it. It was costing me everything I could make to take care of my family. But I made up my mind that I would never again be in a position where I could not tithe.

God wants you to get to a point where you can support the ministry of the Gospel; however, you cannot do it if you do not have the finances.

The Lord cannot speak to you and say give $10,000 to a particular ministry if you do not have the money to give.

He wants His people to be in a position where they will have it to give. God has a financial plan for His people; that plan is tithes and offerings.

There are still too many Christians who are not yet tithers. Some cannot afford to tithe. We hear people say, "You cannot afford *not* to tithe." Well, that is true, but first you have to get into a position to do it. God does not want you to tithe to the neglect of your other financial responsibilities. For example, God does not want you to tithe and then let a company repossess your car or foreclose on your house. God gets no glory out of a situation like that.

God does not want you in bondage. If you never gave a dime, God would still be God. Heaven's streets of gold would not turn into rust, the pearly gates would not fall off their hinges and God would not be out of business if we do not tithe. When we give, it is not for God's benefit. It is for our benefit, because not a penny that we give goes to heaven. It all stays in the earth-realm. We are the ones who get the benefit of what we give.

When our 10,146-seat FaithDome sanctuary was built, not a dime of what we paid to build it fell out of the sky. The funds came through the hands of God's people. And it is those of us who worship in the FaithDome who receive the benefit from the facility. We also are the ones who benefit from the offerings that we give.

God wants us to be economically independent of the circumstances so that we can be dependent only upon Him. He wants us available to meet the needs of the ministries He has ordained. In other words, God wants you, as a Believer, to support the spreading of the Gospel.

God Has Ordained Prosperity

The first thing you need to know is that God ordained prosperity for His children. The ultimate purpose of prosperity is so that God's work can be done.

The pastor in the average church does not talk about money, even though the Gospel cannot be spread without it. Folk get real embarrassed, and act strange when the subject of money is discussed, yet everything we do costs money. *Everything!*

Many people have lots of dreams about what they would like to achieve in life. I can say with virtual certainty that everything they dream of doing costs money. It is the same with the things of God; no work of God gets done without finances. Only the people of God can take care of Kingdom money matters. God cannot do it from heaven; He can only work through us. But we cannot finance the Kingdom if we do not have the funds, and we won't have the funds if we do not know how to get them. Our enemy Satan has so arranged the world's system that you will have just enough to get by. And most of the time you may not even have that.

The majority of people who work on jobs will struggle all their lives. They go from paycheck to paycheck trying to eke out a living but they can never get to the point where they have a surplus — and a surplus is what it really takes to do the job the way God wants it done.

God is not interested in making the Kingdom operate on handouts. Unfortunately, that is the mentality of many Christians. They give God what is left over. If you look at many ministries around the world, you will see that they

3

operate from a poverty mentality, and that kind of thinking often starts in the pulpit. Because I talk about finances and prosperity a lot, I have been called the "prophet of prosperity." Personally, I like the title. It is what God has called me to do — to teach His people that He wants them prosperous. Too many Christians have a challenge with the idea of material prosperity. They can go along with prospering in every way except financially. It is a shame that they are so ignorant of their covenant rights.

Although some folk do not want me or other ministers of the Gospel to talk about money, they are working for money every day of their lives. I might talk about finances once a week, but they go chasing after it five days a week, eight hours a day! They get highly upset when I spend one hour a week talking about it, but they spend 40 hours a week trying to earn it!

For example: Some folk have heard me say that I think I am worth a million dollars a year in salary, and that made them uncomfortable. They mentioned that another renowned Christian leader has worked diligently over the years and receives very little salary. They became indignant that I would have the nerve to make such a statement. My comment to them was that maybe the other person does not think he is worth a million dollars a year, and that is not my fault. As a man thinks in his heart so is he.

If the presidents of major corporations can earn tens of millions of dollars a year, why can't a Christian? I am not interested in a million dollars for the sake of earning a million dollars. I give away 30 percent of all my income to the Kingdom of God. In order for me to give more, I have to get more.

My heart's desire is to give away a million dollars, but I would have to make more than four million dollars a year to do that. A million dollars will go a long way to helping promote the Gospel. Christians put more money than that into Donald Duck and Mickey Mouse, but they put very little into God's kingdom.

People in the world play the lottery; Christians do not have any business playing the lottery. That is the world's system, not God's system. It is not biblical. But even so, if you won $55 million in the lottery, many millions more were made than you received, because the lottery leaders are not in business to give away anything. They are in business to make money. It is your responsibility to receive the prosperity that God wants for you, but you have to play by His rules in order to receive it.

Let's look at Joshua 1:8:

This Book of the Law shall not depart from your mouth, but you shall meditate in it day and night, that you may observe to do according to all that is written in it. For then you will make your way prosperous, and then you will have good success.

According to this verse, you should never stop speaking God's Word. That means God's Word ought to be a part of your everyday life. The purpose of observing is to do; not just observing to observe.

This Scripture does not say that after you observe to do, then God will make your way prosperous. It said *you* will. You are responsible for your own prosperity.

God has done all He is going to do about prosperity. He has already provided it. How much gold do you think is going to fall from the sky and go into the ground tomorrow? It is already there. How much oil is going to fall from the sky and go into the ground? None. It is already there.

The verse says **you will have *good* success**. That is excellent! You could not say it any better than that. There is *good* success, but there is also *bad* success. You are not experiencing good success if you make $10 million a year and your kids are on drugs. You are not experiencing good success if your family is torn asunder. Your net worth according to the world might be phenomenal, but you are miserable. Your kids are running wild. Your husband (or wife) is sleeping at one end of the chateau and you are sleeping at the other, and the twain never meet. That is not good success.

Compared to other people, you might be considered successful, regardless, but it is not good success when you are miserable and have no peace of mind, or when you do not know who your friends are, or when you do not know whether somebody likes you or likes what you have.

Drug kings are successful, moneywise, but that is not good success. Good success is not only having financial and material wealth, but having the peace of mind, joy, and the assurance that your name is written in the Lamb's Book of Life. Good success is having your family and your children together and experiencing love and peace and harmony in the home. God wants us to be prosperous and to have good success.

Psalm 1:1-3:

> **Blessed is the man**
> **Who walks not in the counsel of the ungodly,**
> **Nor stands in the path of sinners,**
> **Nor sits in the seat of the scornful;**
> **But his delight is in the law of the** Lord,
> **And in His law he meditates day and night.**
> **He shall be like a tree**
> **Planted by the rivers of water,**
> **That brings forth its fruit in its season,**
> **Whose leaf also shall not wither;**
> **And whatever he does shall prosper.**

From that passage of Scripture it seems that God wants us to prosper. That is why I do not pay any attention to those who criticize me when it comes to prosperity, because the Word of God says I *should* prosper. Those who criticize do not know any better.

He shall be like a tree planted.... God could have said "he shall be like a tree..." Almost everybody knows what a tree is. But He says, **a tree planted by the rivers of water.** That is important because the tree planted can draw nutrients from the ground. It can draw water from the ground and it can be sustained.

It says **that brings forth its fruit in its season**. You will not bring forth fruit if you are not planted. So with these Scriptures alone, it is clear that God wants us to prosper.

No Great Value in Struggling

A lot of people want to prosper, but somehow they have this idea that God wants them to struggle and that there is some intrinsic value in struggling and just barely making it.

You really have to fight to clear your mind of that kind of thinking so that you are in position to receive God's abundance and prosperity. Some people have the notion that it is spiritual to struggle, because if you have too much, you might forget about God.

That kind of thinking comes from the devil. How in the world could you walk into your palatial house upon the hill that is paid for, and forget about God? If you have a Rolls-Royce sitting in front of the house that is paid for, how in the world could you forget God? He is the one who gave those things to you.

The devil has cheated Christians for years with the phony idea that you will forget God if you become too prosperous.

There is no way I can ever walk in my closet and see my suits hanging there and forget that God provided them for me. How can I forget the Lord? You have money in your pocket. How are you going to forget God?

When I look at my watch, I have to remember God. God moved on the heart of someone to give it to me. I did not pay a dime for it. I went to the jewelry store and the man looked at the watch and said, that watch costs $8,500. Yet, somebody gave it to me.

The devil has tricked Christians out of what they ought to have.

Again now, the ultimate purpose is to finance the Kingdom of God. But in the process of financing the Kingdom, you can get the things you need and want. That just goes with the territory. Actually, you could live off the fringe benefits.

God wants you to prosper both financially and in your
home. So, if you are not prospering, there is something you
can do about it. You can break the power of the devil in
your home.

If you are raising your children and living in line with
the Word of God, none of your children should be on alcohol or drugs. There is no need to get in bondage because
other people did not know the Word and did not know how
to raise their children. When you come into a knowledge of
the Word and learn you have some authority, you can do
something about those things spiritually.

You do not have to sit around saying, "Oh, my poor
child is on cocaine." You can start exerting a spiritual influence over the demon of cocaine. You can turn the situation
around. You do not have to give up and say, "Well, that's
cocaine, and once that cocaine gets you, there is no hope."
That is a lie. Do not let anybody tell you that. That is the
devil telling you that. Cocaine is nothing! It is a deception
of the devil.

God's Word will work for you. He wants you prosperous in every area of life. But that means you cannot fellowship with sinners, shack up with them, live with them, go
into business with them and expect the Word to work.

You have to delight yourself in the law of the Lord.
You have to meditate on His Word day and night. Usually
when you hear the word *meditate*, you think of sitting down
and quietly thinking. But the word in Hebrew really means
"to utter or mutter."

Third John 2 says:

> **Beloved, I pray that you may prosper in all
> things and be in health, just as your soul prospers.**

9

You can never function in God's financial plan until you get to the point where you have your thinking straight about the fact that God wants you to prosper. Once you get everything in proper perspective, you can have it all.

When you read that Scripture about prospering, it is talking about materially, physically and spiritually. Prosperity is the natural outcome of meditating in the Word and doing the Word as God said. The prosperity will take care of itself.

Here is an example of what I mean: If you put a pan of water on the stove and turn the burner up, boiling is automatic. If you never put water on the burner or over heat, you will never have boiling water. The point is that there are certain things you have to do if you want boiling water. First of all, you have to get a container. Second, you have to put water in the container. Third, you have to put the container on a heat source. All those things must be done to get into a position to have boiling water. So, in like fashion, prosperity is the natural result and outcome of walking by the Word.

Steps Toward Good Success

Success with God comes from finding out what He requires of you, then getting in line with that, being obedient to it and not letting anything or anybody deter you from accomplishing that goal.

When the FaithDome was under construction, there was contention from all quarters. People criticized, saying, "You spent all that money on that great big building. Think about all the hungry folk out there. You're right in the middle of the ghetto and you spent all that money on a building. Think about how many people you could have fed."

It is important not to let anything sidetrack you when you are doing what you believe God told you to do. But if you are not careful, you will allow your human feelings rather than the Lord to direct your actions. When you do that, you compromise your assignment, the anointing lifts off, and you are then on your own, doing things in your own strength and your own ability. You cannot afford to do that.

It cost a lot of money to build the FaithDome. We could have taken the $12 million to buy $12 million worth of food for the hungry and provided the grandest meal that they had ever eaten in their whole lives. But when the meal was over, they would have been hungry the next day, and the $12 million would have been gone.

I believe in feeding the hungry. I believe in providing where there is a need. But this is God's business, and ministers make a mistake when they mix up their personal feelings with the things of God, attempting to use God's resources to meet what they want to do. That's a trap, because what God is about is much bigger than a few hungry people.

That could sound cold and callous, but if you accuse me of being uncaring and callous, you would have to accuse God of that as well. God has more resources than Fred Price does. He knows about all the starving people around the world, and He is not lifting a finger to do anything for them. Why not tell God He is unrighteous and unkind?

Why doesn't He feed all these people who are starving around the world? What most people do not understand is that there is a reason for those people starving, and if you never deal with the reason, they are going to starve the rest of their lives. The reason is that those starving people, for the most part, either do not know Jesus as their personal Savior and Lord, or they do not know God has a plan that can release them from the bondage of poverty.

Many Christians think that things just work helter-skelter or haphazardly. But God does have a plan, and we as the children of God can get involved with that plan. As a result of getting involved, the needs of ministries such as mine at Crenshaw Christian Center will be met in the earth-realm.

Chicken Dinners, Rummage Sales

God's way of meeting the needs of ministry is not through chicken dinners or rummage sales. You do not find bingo games in God's Word either. Yet, if you look around, over the years, this is what many churches and ministries have resorted to: gimmicks and games to finance the Kingdom of God.

Salvation is freely offered to us. All we have to do is by faith receive it. But getting the message of salvation to people, along with teaching them about the victorious lifestyle in Christ that accompanies it, costs a lot of money. Christians easily understand that it costs money to buy gasoline to operate their cars and to pay taxes and put a roof over their heads, but they have no problem understanding that clothing their bodies costs money. When it comes to the Gospel, somehow they have this weird idea that the money will just fall out of the sky from heaven.

TWO

THE WORLD
SYSTEM'S PROSPERITY

When we as Christians give an offering or pay the tithe, we give it as unto the Lord. He, on the other hand, gives us credit for giving to Him, but the money really benefits us. It provides all the things we need to spread the Gospel.

Only the people of God are going to support the proclamation of the Gospel. To do that, we have to have the resources. And where will we get the resources? We have to get them through God's financial plan, because we will never get ahead by punching a clock and drawing a salary.

The world system is not designed for us to get ahead, because if we ever become financially independent of our circumstances, we will be uncontrollable.

How much influence do the powers that be exert over Donald Trump? They do not tell him what to do. He and others like him pretty well tell the government what to do. That is the way it is. Money speaks.

When you become financially independent, you are very difficult to deal with, because on Monday morning, you might decide to go yachting instead of going to the plant. You might decide to take a trip and go skiing instead of working on the computer. So a system has been devised to keep you at the wheels of industry so that those who are in positions of authority and the super-rich can enjoy the fruits of your labor.

The system is designed for you to make just enough, giving you the illusion of getting ahead. In that way, you will continue to be willing to go to work.

Very few people truly love their work and look forward to going to their jobs with a great thrill and anticipation. Most people go to work out of necessity. If they do not go to work, they are going to starve. If the powers-that-be did not figure out a way to keep people at the wheels of industry, nobody would work and there would be no manufactured goods. And the rich would not be able to sit back and be served.

God wants you to be free and independent of the circumstances, so that you can freely give to support the Gospel.

God has a plan for you to become financially independent of the circumstances. In order to get into that plan, you have to first know that God wants you to prosper.

God's Covenant With Man

The Bible tells us that God gives us power to get wealth. That lets you know God is not opposed to wealth. But you have to keep your priorities in the right perspective, and

14

remember that the purpose of the wealth is to establish His covenant. Now what does "establish His covenant" mean?

I believe it means exactly what Jesus said when He said, "I came that you might have life, and have it more abundantly." God's covenant with man is abundant life and abundant living, because God does not need anything. He is not on welfare.

We are the ones who have needs, and God has provided a way for those needs to be met. All that is a part of the salvation that Jesus came to bring us. Most of the time we think being a Christian means missing hell when we die and going to heaven. That is true and wonderful, but that is not all God has for you. He has abundance for you, so that the world can have the Gospel proclaimed to it and come out of bondage and into the light and into the wonders of God's great plan and purpose.

We have looked at Joshua 1:8, Psalm 1:1-3, and 3 John 2 to establish the fact that God wants us to prosper. Let us now look at Psalm 35:27:

> **Let them shout for joy and be glad,**
> **Who favor my righteous cause;**
> **And let them say continually,**
> **"Let the LORD be magnified,**
> **Who has pleasure in the prosperity of His**
> **servant."**

We are the children of God, but at the same time, we are also called the servants of the Lord. We are His servants in that we do His bidding. Jesus is the head. The Church is the body.

HIGHER FINANCE

Your body is the servant of your head. If your head says, "I want some Swiss Almond Vanilla ice cream," your head directs your feet and your feet head to the freezer. Your head tells your hand, "Reach up and take the handle of the freezer, pull it toward you. Reach your hand in and go through the strawberry and the vanilla and get the Swiss Almond Vanilla. Pull it out and close the freezer door." Your head is directing your body. Your head cannot go in there and get that ice cream, so your head has a servant — your body.

Likewise, we, the Body of Christ, are the servants of the Lord. Jesus is seated at the right hand of the Father in heaven. He is not opening the refrigerator or the freezer, but the body, the arms, the hands, the limbs, are the servants of the Lord.

The verse says the Father takes "pleasure" in our prosperity. What is the opposite of pleasure? Displeasure. If the Lord has pleasure in the prosperity of His servants, He must have displeasure in the poverty of His servants. You would have to be totally unintelligent to misunderstand that. It is very clear that God does want us to be prosperous.

God has given us role models in His Word. There were some very prosperous role models in the Bible. Why do we need role models? Basically to inspire and encourage us. We see somebody else winning and it inspires us to at least think we can win. We see somebody successful and it encourages us to think we can be successful.

Through the characters in the Bible, God has shown us that we can win. He wants us to succeed. But all those great role models did not stop with Abraham, Isaac, Samson, Joshua and other great men of the Bible. What about the role models in the generations that followed? What about us

16

today? God wants us to write new chapters, so to speak, stories about conquering and succeeding.

I like winners. I like to read about and hang around winners. I do not want to read a story about how to fail. I know how to fail. You do not have to go to school to learn how to fail. All you have to do for about 60 days is stay in bed and you will be a failure. Never get up and never go to work and you will fail.

We see failure all around us all the time, but what we do not see is God-quality success. We see devilish, satanic-quality success. We see how the devil's kids succeed, but we really do not have that many role models from a spiritual point of view who will dare to stand up and say, "I am where I am because of Jesus Christ. I am a success because of the power of the Holy Spirit."

The devil has tricked people into believing that they are not supposed to be victorious, not supposed to be prosperous. But we should not settle for second best on anything. No matter how small the matter might seem, we should be and have the best.

We feel we are doing something wrong when we aspire to the best, because the world system is constantly reminding us that we are not supposed to prosper as Christians. On the other hand, it is great if people in the world get on top and become prosperous because it is the devil's territory.

We have to go almost overboard with the subject of prosperity and become fanatical with it in order for Christians to understand prosperity is their right. We have to go almost overboard to get it into their hearts that they should prosper so that the covenant of God can be established.

Deuteronomy 8:18:

"And you shall remember the LORD your God, for it is He who gives you power to get wealth, that He may establish His covenant which He swore to your fathers, as it is this day."

Galatians 3:13-14:

Christ has redeemed us from the curse of the law, having become a curse for us (for it is written, *"Cursed is everyone who hangs on a tree"*),
that the blessings of Abraham might come upon the Gentiles in Christ Jesus, that we might receive the promise of the Spirit through faith.

The Bible uses Abraham as an example and a symbol of a man of faith. We who are children of God have received our salvation and our sonship with God through faith. So, we are faith people.

Look at Galatians 3:7:

Therefore know that *only* those who are of faith are sons of Abraham.

You would think it would say that they "are the children of God." Why do you suppose it says, "the children of Abraham"? Abraham is not our father. I thought God was our father once we became His children. But Abraham is being used as a role model of a man of faith, because Abraham believed God.

Throughout time, God has used Abraham as a paragon of faith and virtue and as an example to us.

18

Look at Galatians 3:9:

So then those who *are* of faith are blessed with believing Abraham.

I like that. Now if that is true and God cannot lie, then what we need to do is to find out how Abraham was blessed, then we will know how we are supposed to be blessed. If Abraham was blessed spiritually, then we know we should be blessed spiritually. If Abraham was blessed soulishly, we know we should be blessed soulishly as well. If Abraham was blessed materially and physically, then that is the way we should be blessed.

This information is foundational for your understanding of God's financial plan and your covenant rights to prosperity. And it is important to lay an accurate, substantial foundation so that you have something to build on. And that way, no one can talk you out of what you know.

Oftentimes, the devil talks people out of things because they do not have a good foundation in the Word of God. They believe it because it sounds good, or they heard someone say it. They have confidence in another person's word. That's fine, but they need to see it in the Word of God for themselves.

When it comes time to do battle, I do not go out in the name of Fred Price or anyone else. I go out in the name of Jesus, based on what the Lord says in the Word, and that is what will put you over.

Now look at Genesis 12:1:

Now the LORD had said unto Abram: "Get out of your country,

19

**From your family
And from your father's house,
To a land that I will show you."**

Originally, Abraham's name was Abram — which means "father of the nation," singular. Later on, after faithfully walking with God, God changed his name to Abraham, which means "father of the nations," plural — more than one.

God is God to those who are not in the family. But to those in the family, He's Father. The Father God is in the business of creating and unifying the family. But God told Abraham to get out of his earthly father's house, and away from his familiar surroundings; leave his country, leave his city and go to a place that "I will show you."

He told him to leave his relatives. What was God doing? Well, sometimes, if you are going to walk in the way of the Lord, you will have to leave family. And if you stay, they will drag you down to their level. It can be heart-rending and traumatic to leave family. But you have a choice — to please family or to please your heavenly Father. Because if you will be willing and obedient, you shall eat the good of the land.

Not only will you eat the good of the land, but God will give you a bigger family. He will give you so many family members, so many brothers and sisters, you will not be able to count them. He will give you people who will love you just like your blood relatives love you; people who will protect you and stand up for you and fight for you and take care of you — sometimes even better than family members will — because they are loving you with the love of the Lord, not with just a selfish, blood-love relationship.

But God told Abraham to get out, leave his people and go out into **a land that I will show you.** Leaving family and familiar surroundings is what it takes sometimes to follow God and to do what He says. You have to stand by yourself and you will never be victorious or truly successful until you are ready to make that kind of commitment.

Sometimes you have to pull up stakes and go where you don't want to go. You would rather not go, but if you want to stay in the perfect will of God you will go and you will be blessed as a result of it. Because God is working something out in you, and He cannot work it out where you are. He has to get you away where you will be free from a particular situation. But He may send you right back where you came from, and by returning there you will change what is there. However, you have to get changed first.

Genesis 12:2-3:

> **"I will make you a great nation;**

I will bless you
> **And make your name great;**
> **And you shall be a blessing.**
> **I will bless those who bless you,**
> **And I will curse him who curses you;**
> **And in you all the families of the earth shall be**
blessed."

How then does God bless people? He blesses people through people. You cannot be a blessing until you are blessed yourself.

God had to have another man by which He could get back into this world and get that blessing back to the people of God; He did it through Abraham. He never said this of any other man: He said, I will bless you and then I will cause you to be a blessing. Abraham is called the "father of the faithful." So everybody who is exercising faith in Jesus Christ, and in the Word of God, are typed along with Abraham.

Genesis 13:1-2:

> **Then Abram went up from Egypt, he and his wife and all that he had, and Lot with him, to the South.**
> **Abram was very rich in livestock, in silver, and in gold.**

Notice what it does not say; it does not simply say that Abraham was rich. It says that Abraham was *very* rich. *Very* rich means that his rich was rich!

THREE

A HEAVENLY BANK ACCOUNT

W e have a heavenly bank account and we should learn how to make deposits and withdrawals from the account.

Matthew 6:19-21:

> **"Do not lay up for yourselves treasures on earth, where moth and rust destroy and where thieves break in and steal;**
>
> **"but lay up for yourselves treasures in heaven, where neither moth nor rust destroys and where thieves do not break in and steal.**
>
> **"For where your treasure is, there your heart will be also."**

If you are not careful, you will get the idea that Jesus is saying that we should have neither a bank account nor a savings account, nor should we invest money. In other words, we should not accumulate any of this world's goods, but simply reserve enough money to live on today because we are not supposed to lay up for ourselves treasures on earth. But you have to understand that this particular segment of Scripture is really not talking about treasure as such; it is talking about a condition of the heart.

We have to disengage our mind from the traditional way of thinking that God is opposed to "treasure," as well as that His definition is the same as ours about what constitutes treasure in this earth life. He is dealing with our hearts.

If your heart is right, your life will be right. You cannot have a right heart and a wrong life. That does not fit. The tree is known by its fruit. You cannot have a lemon tree producing grapefruit. You cannot have an apple tree producing walnuts.

Whatever is on the inside is what is going to come out on the branches. If your treasure — in other words, if your heart is on earthly things, then it is not in the things of the Kingdom of God. As a result, your lifestyle is not going to be commensurate with the things of God, but with those things where your heart is. So then your life's aspirations become the pursuit and the acquisition of material things.

We should use material things simply as tools to meet our needs and to be channels of blessings to meet the needs of the Kingdom of God.

God is not opposed to wealth, because He is rich. But He is opposed to our having our hearts in the riches rather than in the Kingdom. If we get our hearts in the Kingdom, we can handle the riches.

A lot of times we see where rich people have squandered their money. If our hearts are in the Kingdom of God, we are not going to waste riches. We will want to keep an account of every penny we get because we know that we are stewards before God, and are going to have to give an account of our stewardship. The Bible says, "To whom much is given, of him shall much be required." So if $50 million come into your hands, God is going to require more out of you than He would from somebody who has $50.

Ephesians 1:3:

Blessed be the God and Father of our Lord Jesus Christ, who has blessed us with every spiritual blessing in the heavenly places in Christ.

Keep in mind that the Book of Ephesians is written to the people of God, not to people in general. So when it says, "... who has blessed us," it means us Christians, us children of God, us born-again people.

The origin of everything is first spiritual. Why? Because God, who is a spirit, created all things. If God, who is a spirit, created all things, then all things at their source must be spiritual. If they came out of God, they have to have some of God in them. The things that God creates have to come out of a spirit or a spiritual foundation. Can you understand that?

In the beginning, God created the heavens and the earth. The earth is material, but God, a spirit, created it. Therefore the material earth is dependent upon a spirit for its existence.

Television, radio, airplanes, automobiles, watches, jewelry, houses, furniture, clothing, shoes, boats, etc. — all came from the Spirit.

Satan, who is a usurper, has prostituted these things and made them available for the world rather than the children

25

of God. He tricked the Church into thinking it wasn't for them. So Christians shied away from those things and that has allowed Satan to gather them, distribute them among his children and keep them out of the hands of the children of God.

If God's people ever get those material riches into their hands, they will be able to fulfill the covenant of God and the Gospel can be spread through the world without a hindrance anywhere. Because, even though salvation is offered as a free gift, it costs a lot of money to get it to those who need it.

When the Gospel is spread, people will no longer live in ignorance of God's plan and purpose. They will know what belongs to them. They will know they are already blessed. And they will know about God's financial plan for them.

I am already blessed, so I should expect that blessings would manifest in my life. In other words, if I am doing all the other things that constitute a right heart toward God and His Word, God will allow the channel of my life to be open so that the things that He has already blessed me with can come to me.

If you could go back in my life 30 years ago, before I found out about the Word and how to walk by faith, before I found out that I was already blessed, before I found out that I had a covenant, before I found out that I could be filled with the Spirit, before I found out that I could operate in God's plenty, before I found out that I was supposed to be blessed with faithful Abraham, you would see that I was a wreck going somewhere to happen.

Thirty years ago I was struggling, but today I do not struggle. All my needs are met. My needs were not met 30 years ago, even though I was the same and God was the same and there was the same money out in circulation that is in circulation today. Yet I did not have any money — and I did not know how to get any.

Today is a different story. People walk up to me and hand me money. People send me money personally. They say, "This is for you and your wife. We want you to go to dinner." It happens all the time. Or people just walk up to me and say, "The Lord told me to give you this." Nobody did that 30 years ago. They did not give me anything but a hard way to go and a hard way to get there.

If God is the same yesterday and today and forever, then it was His will back then and it is His will today for me to prosper. Ephesians 1:3 was in the Bible 20, 30, 50 years ago. All during the time I was struggling, Ephesians was in the Bible, but I wasn't operating in it. Why? Because my treasure was not in heaven. My treasure was down here trying to get enough money to pay the bills and keep the economic wolf off my front porch.

One of my favorite verses was Matthew 6:33, which says: **"seek first the kingdom of God and His righteousness...."** I used to read and quote the verse, but I did not know how to do it. God said if I seek Him first, all these other things would be added. Man, they were taking stuff away from me! They were repossessing the car and the television and calling for me to return their credit cards.

God said these thing would be added, not subtracted. So something was wrong. Do not misunderstand me, my heart was right as far as desiring to live the God kind of life, but I did not know how to lay up for myself treasures in heaven. I thought I had to get them here in the earth-realm.

I was going after them with my ability and my strength, and because I was a child of God, the devil was cheating me every step of the way. I was not a worldly person. If I were a worldly person, I might have been able to make millions of dollars. But Satan does not want the children of God to get that kind of money because they will use it against him.

When I found out about laying up for myself treasures in heaven, and about seeking first the Kingdom, and when I found out I was supposed to be blessed so that I could be a blessing, and I started walking in that and operating in that, my circumstances began to change. It did not happen instantaneously, but it happened a lot faster than it did for me to get into the mess. I started getting out much quicker than I got into it.

Life was handing me a raw deal in those earlier years. Why? Because I wasn't doing what God said to do. I didn't know what I was supposed to do in order to do what God said to do?

The churches I went to did not tell me what I was supposed to do. I thought I was supposed to get out there and struggle the best way I could and exhibit a Christian lifestyle.

I did not know I was already blessed. When I found that out, I began calling the blessings in and doing what God said to do, and it was almost a miracle how my life changed. It almost looked as if God started taking a liking to me. It almost looked as if God fell in love with me, when all those other times it seemed as if He didn't like me too well. All of a sudden, it seemed as if "God likes Fred!" and He started blessing me. No! He did not start blessing; the blessings were already there.

The Law of God's Word

What I did was get in line with the flow of God's Word, and when you get in line with the flow, the flow will get in line with you. When you turn the water on in the shower, you can walk all around the outside of the shower and never get a drop of water on you. But when you walk into the shower, you are going to get wet, because that is where water is falling — inside the shower.

God's blessings are just like the water falling in the shower. If you want to get in the water, you have to get inside the shower and let the water fall on you, and that is what I started doing.

God never changed. I changed. Instead of standing outside the shower, I got in it and the blessings that were already flowing out of the pipeline of God got on me. I started laying up for myself treasures in heaven. I started doing what God said to do.

I wanted to lay this practical foundation before I begin telling you how to actually lay up for yourself treasures in heaven.

Why do you think Jesus said to lay up for yourself treasures in heaven?

The reason is because earthly treasures are subject to earthly conditions. When you lay up for yourself treasures in heaven, it is not affected by earthly conditions.

Let me give you a good example of how earthly conditions change: I have been married for more than 45 years. When I first got married, my wife and I bought a week's groceries for $10 and we ate well. You could buy a tin of those pop-out biscuits for 10 cents — a dime! For a dollar you would have enough biscuits to last for a couple of months.

You can hardly buy anything for $10 now, let alone $1. Buy washing detergent, bleach, toilet paper, a bar of soap, and you have blown $12. Forty years ago, gasoline cost 16 cents a gallon. Earthly treasure is affected by earthly conditions. You have to have 25 times as much money today to do the same things that you could do 40 years ago with $1.

If you learn how to lay up for yourself treasures in heaven, your dollar in heaven will have 100-cent value, where on earth it does not. The value is always changing on earth, depending upon the economic trend of the times. Because of earthly conditions, you could have a million dollars in the bank today and be broke next week — depending on where your money is invested.

If your heart is in the economic system, you are going to do what some people did during the last stock market crash — kill themselves, jump out of windows. Why? Because their heart is in their money, that is where their treasure is. And when that treasure changes, because it is affected by earthly conditions, they go bananas. Earthly conditions blow them away.

Jesus does not want us to get hung up on material things. Whether a dollar is worth 5 cents, 25 cents, 100 cents or 110 cents, it does not make any difference if your heart is in the right place. And if you need $10,000 more than you would have needed 40 years ago, God will provide it, if you learn how to operate in His flow.

FOUR

A SPIRIT OF POVERTY

I like to bring things out in the open so that people can be free. I know preachers won't like what I'm about to say, but there is a spirit of poverty that manifests itself in the material physical world.

There is no reason for poverty because there is no shortage of wealth. There really is no need for anybody to be poor. But the spirit of poverty has so conditioned certain people's minds that they have allowed themselves to be divested of what God Almighty intended for them.

Money has been allowed to flow into the hands of a few men around the world who continue to keep the money away from others.

I was reading a magazine article about the richest people in the world. There was a story of a man who lived on the island of Borneo who was worth $34 billion — at least this is what he allows people to know. He lived in a palace that costs $300 million. With that kind of money you could buy 3,000 houses for 3,000 homeless people and pay cash for

31

them! That's what you call money. And this man is making money by the millions just by having money in the bank. Imagine what the tithe would be off of $34 billion! You could do a lot for the Kingdom of God.

Once again, this proves my point that there is no shortage of wealth. If you were to take all the other wealthy people in the world and divide all the money up, there would be plenty for everybody.

There is plenty of food, plenty of money, and plenty of everything else. Yet there are people who are starving. Why? Because there is a demon spirit in this world that gets into the minds of people.

There is a spirit of poverty that works through the Church and operates from the pulpit, a demon spirit that infiltrates the minds of ministers and convinces them that they are supposed to be poor and not have any of this world's goods. In other words, Christians should have just enough to make it. That poverty spirit cheats the people of God out of what rightfully belongs to them.

Let's find out what God's attitude is about poverty. Let's read 1 Timothy 6:17 (this is God speaking through the mouth of his servant, Paul):

> **Command those who are rich in this present age not to be haughty, nor to trust in uncertain riches but in the living God, who gives us richly all things to enjoy.**

Who is this being written to — the world or the Body of Christ?

That Scripture has to be talking about rich Christians, because this letter is not written to sinners, and Christians have no authority to tell sinners what to do with their wealth. What constitutes rich in this world? Money. Basically, when we say *rich* we mean money and everything that money can buy and everything that money can do.

There used to be a TV show called *Lifestyles of the Rich & Famous*. And when that program came on, it would never take you to the ghetto or to Skid Row. You would never see a beat-up tent with a tin roof on *Lifestyles of the Rich & Famous*. They would take you to mansions with great big iron gates that open electronically, with driveways that are four miles long. You did not go to a ghetto shack.

God does not say get rid of the riches; He just says don't trust in them. Why? Because they are uncertain. The same thing Jesus said when He said not to lay up treasures on earth, because the thieves are going to get it — the political thieves as well as the kind of thieves who break into your house and steal what is yours. He tells us to trust in the living God.

We have been lied to by the religious establishment. It is that demon spirit of poverty that has operated through religion to cheat us out of what belongs to us.

Christians ought to be among the rich in this world, and I am one who is working toward it. I do not want to be rich simply for the sake of being rich, but so that I can be a channel of blessing for God to be able to establish His covenant. But I cannot give what I do not have, so I have to get it first so I can give it. The devil is not going to give it to me; I am going to have to take it by faith.

The Basis of God's Financial Plan

Tithes and offerings are the very center and circumference of God's financial plan. Again, the issue is not the money, it is the condition of your heart. Where is your heart?

While on our way to church one rainy Sunday morning, my wife and I saw a man jogging. From the looks of it, keeping his flesh intact was important. His flesh was possibly his treasure, and he was taking care of it come hell or high water, rain, sleet, snow or sunshine. He should have been in church, but he was laying up physical bodily treasure for himself. Maybe he had gone to church earlier, but one could think what my wife and I thought about the situation — that his flesh was very important to him — possibly his treasure.

Jesus is the one who made the silver, the diamonds, the pearls, so you know God is not opposed to material treasure. He is the one who invented it. Some people think the Father God made the silver and gold, but Jesus made them. I did not say He created them, I said He is the one who made them.

The Bible says that in the beginning God created the heavens and the earth. But what are they composed of? Our scientists tell us a commodity called matter is the building block, or the ingredients that everything else is made of. So God created the matter, but Jesus shaped it and formed it into what we see now. That means that God created the matter that gold is made out of, but Jesus made gold, iron, copper, diamonds, sapphires, and all the other things.

John 1:1-3:

> **In the beginning was the Word, and the Word was with God, and the Word was God.**
> **He was in the beginning with God.**
> **All things were made through Him, and without Him nothing was made that was made.**

It doesn't say *created*, but it says "made." Can you see that? God was the one who created the building materials, but Jesus was the architect.

There is a difference between the words *make* and *create*. To create in its most technical meaning is the ability to bring something out of nothing, to start from zero and make something or produce something. Only God can create.

Each year when the seasons change, the designers in the clothing industry talk about the fall creations. They are not really creations, they are taking pre-existing material and just shaping it in a new way, dyeing it a different color, but it is the same old material, same old yarn, same old silk, etc.

God is the creator; Jesus was the architect who designed everything we see; the Holy Spirit energized it and gave it life.

God is the creator, Jesus is the maker, and the Holy Spirit is the sustainer or the power source.

I mention all of that so you will know all the earthly goods originated from a spiritual source, and since this is the case, God cannot be opposed to your having those things. He just wants you to have your heart set on Him and not on the earthly things He created.

If you get yourself heavenly minded, you will become some earthly good. But if you get yourself earthly minded, then you won't be any heavenly good or spiritually good.

Although we have a heavenly bank account, God wants us to make deposits in the spirit world, and out of those spiritual deposits, they will return and manifest themselves through our lives in material ways, but our hearts won't be wrapped up materialistically. And that is the thing that God is concerned with and that is what Jesus was getting across to us.

Your Security Is in Heaven

I could take a $5 bill and deposit it in my earthly bank account. That is on earth. When He says "lay up for yourself treasures in heaven," He could not be talking about $5 bills, because you could not get one up to heaven if you wanted to. He does not want us to set our hearts on $5 bills. He did not say you could not have them, but when your heart is set on them you will steal, kill and take them away from others. You will con people out of them, you will embezzle. That kind of thing can happen when your heart is in it.

Some people — even though they do not or cannot have certain things — still covet them. So their hearts are still in those things even though they do not have them, because if they had a chance to get these things, they sure would take it and leave everything else on the side, including God. And Jesus knows that.

First Timothy 6:17 says:

Command those who are rich in this present age not to be haughty, nor to trust in uncertain

riches but in the living God, who gives us richly all things to enjoy.

That is the key and that is the challenge. The problem is the *trusting* in the riches. He is telling this to Christians. He could not be telling unsaved people not to trust in their wealth, because for the non-Christian, trusting in their wealth is normal; wealth is their god.

The unbelievers are not about to give up their riches. They are trying to get more all the time. What God is saying to Christians is, **Command those who *are* rich.** He makes this so plain you would have to hire somebody to help you misunderstand this. He said **rich in this world....** That is not talking about heaven; that is talking about this world.

What happens sometimes with the rich folk is that they are high-minded. They begin thinking they are bigger than the law. They think they can get away with anything. They can park in the red no-parking zones. They can go to the head of the line. They think they should have special treatment; after all, they're rich.

You can get haughty and high-minded if you are not careful. You will think you are God. And in this world system you *are* God if you have enough money, because you can buy people's lives and even end them.

So Paul could not be telling sinners not to trust in their riches because this is all they have to trust in. They cannot trust in God. They do not even believe in God or know Him. So 1 Timothy 6:17 has to be talking about Christian people. The letter is written to Christians.

I learn a lot of things when I read the Bible. And I often learn by reading what it does not say. When I read what it does not say, it makes what it does say explode in revelation. Notice, Paul does not say, "Command those who are rich in this present age to give up their riches." He does not tell them to get rid of their wealth. What he tells them to do is to not be haughty and to not trust in their riches.

If your heart is not set on things, then from a spiritual point of view, the things of earth do not control you. If someone does break in and steals all your money, it would not cost you even one minute of concern, because your heart is not set on earthly things. It would not cause you a minute's strife. You would not even be concerned about it because you would know there is more where that came from.

You know what the word *richly* means? In the Greek it means "abundant," "abundantly," and "copiously" and "lavishly supplied." That's what it means.

He says "who gives us richly all things to enjoy." That word *enjoy* is another interesting word in the Greek. It carries the idea "to take hold of," "to enjoy a thing." It suggests "the advantage or pleasure to be obtained from a thing." That is what it actually means in the Greek. Right away, Christians will get scared of this. They might say, "Aw, my God. That man, I knew he was worldly. Listen to him talk about 'enjoy' things." But I did not write this.

All this is based upon the fact that you have laid up your treasures in heaven. Your heart is not set on things.

For unsaved rich people, their heart is in their wealth. Let's look at 1 Timothy 6:18:

Let them do good, that they be rich in good works, ready to give, willing to share.

38

Do you know that you can do more good with a million dollars than you can with five dollars? We can do good with money — when it is in the right hands. He did not tell us to get rid of it, he said, do good. Think about how many hungry people you could feed with a million dollars.

There are enough rich people in the world to do away with poverty. Unsaved rich people could get rid of poverty if they would pool their resources. They could not only give somebody a home or a place to stay or food and clothing, but they could create jobs. They could build factories. They could do all kinds of positive things.

How much are the rich doing today to alleviate poverty? Not much. They give some money to certain schools, universities, endowments, and things like that, but so much more could be done. Doing something for somebody's life is more important than placing a statue in the park.

The poor cannot help themselves. I am not saying that poor people cannot do better; what I am saying is that one poor man cannot do much for another poor man, but they can do *something* for themselves. They can listen to the Word. If they would listen to the Word, they would not be poor anymore, because there is no shortage of wealth in God. Wealth, like help, is available from the Lord.

The word *rich* in Verse 18 means "wealthy." It means "wealthy in good works."

Mark 4:14-19

"The sower sows the word.

"And these are the ones by the wayside where the word is sown. When they hear, Satan comes

immediately and takes away the word that was sown in their hearts.

" These likewise are the ones sown on stony ground who, when they hear the word, immediately receive it with gladness;

"and they have no root in themselves, and so endure only for a time. Afterward, when tribulation or persecution arises for the word's sake, immediately they stumble.

"Now these are the ones sown among thorns; they are the ones who hear the word,

"and the cares of this world, the deceitfulness of riches, and the desires for other things entering in choke the word, and it becomes unfruitful."

Notice right in the middle of that last verse the words the deceitfulness of riches.

What choked the Word? He said the deceitfulness of riches choked the Word, *not the riches*. There is a difference there.

"... and the desires for other things entering in choke the word."

He did not even say other things were the problem. He said, the *desires* for or the *lust* of other things. It is the lust that causes a person to hit a man in the head and take his things. It is the lust that causes men to break in somebody's house and take what does not belong to them. Lust will drive you to do things that are beyond reason.

It is beyond reason to break into somebody's house. You do not know who is in that house. You do not know if the guy is sitting there with a sawed-off shotgun, waiting to blow your head off. You take your life into your hands. But lust drives a person beyond reason. The lusts of other things and the deceitfulness of riches. Not *riches*, but the deceitfulness of them.

People become so taken up with the riches that they are deceived by them, because they think nobody can tell them what to do. They feel they can circumvent the law because they have enough money to buy those who make the laws and who are supposed to enforce the laws. They think they can get them to do what they want because they can offer them money. This is deceit.

When it says that the desires of other things entering in choke the word, that means it hinders and limits the Word from producing, from growing and developing and maturing as it ought to and as God designed it to.

Philippians 4:13 says **I can do all things** [not through me but] **through Christ**. If I can do all things, I can avoid the deceitfulness of riches. If I cannot avoid it, then I cannot do all things and God lied to me. He held out to me the impossible dream. But I *can* do all things through Christ. And this is what the Church has not understood. When I say the *Church*, I mean the leaders of the Church.

Just as you can avoid the deceitfulness of people, you can avoid the deceitfulness of riches. You do not stop interfacing with people, you just avoid their deceit.

You can do all things through Christ who strengthens you, so you do not have to get caught up in the deceitfulness of riches.

We are in control, so we can have and distribute wealth without the deceitfulness of riches controlling us.

People say, "That Fred Price is so materialistic." It is not that. God wants his children to have something and they cannot get it if somebody doesn't tell them. And most people do not have enough guts to do it, because they do not want to be criticized. But criticism doesn't bother me because I know who I am and I am not intimidated.

Hours Spent Seeking Money

God has to get His message of financial prosperity across and very few people are saying much about it. But God cannot get the job done unless He can get us beyond the traditions that have robbed us.

Most of our waking hours are spent acquiring money. On the average, most of us spend more time seeking money than we do eating or sleeping.

People go to school to better themselves, to get into a position to make more money by selling their marketable skills to society.

Just think about how much time you spend making a living. If you did not have to do that you could spend that time, conceivably, studying the Word, ministering the Word of God, talking to people about the things of God. You could spend time praying in the Spirit. But you spend most of your time trying to make money.

And think about all the other time you spend just getting to the place to make the money. You get up early in the morning to get to your eight-hour job. Then you have to leave your workplace, and, again more time is involved in getting home from work. If you add it all up, you spend a lot of time in the acquisition of money.

FIVE

UNCERTAIN RICHES

L et's read Mark 10:17-26:

Now as He was going out on the road, one came
running, knelt before him, and asked Him,
"Good Teacher, what shall I do that I may inherit
eternal life?"

So Jesus said to him, "Why do you call me
good? No one is good but One, that is, God.

"You know the commandments: 'Do not commit adultery,' 'Do not murder,' 'Do not steal,' 'Do
not bear false witness,' 'Do not defraud,' 'Honor
your father and your mother.' "

And he answered and said to Him, "Teacher,
all these things I have kept from my youth."

Then Jesus, looking at him, loved him, and said
to him, "One thing you lack: Go your way, sell
whatever you have and give to the poor, and you
will have treasure in heaven; and come, take up
the cross, and follow Me."

But he was sad at this word, and went away sorrowful, for he had great possessions.

Then Jesus looked around and said to His disciples, "How hard it is for those who have riches to enter the kingdom of God!"

And the disciples were astonished at His words. But Jesus answered again and said to them, "Children, how hard it is for those who trust in riches to enter the kingdom of God!

"It is easier for a camel to go through the eye of a needle than for a rich man to enter the kingdom of God."

And they were greatly astonished, saying among themselves, "Who then can be saved?"

If you stop without reading the entire passage, you may draw the wrong conclusion. You may conclude that because Jesus told him to leave his possessions and follow Him, that Jesus did not want this rich young ruler to have those possessions. Or you may conclude that if you have wealth, you will never get into the Kingdom of God. But neither of these conclusions is accurate.

Jesus had a deeper reason for what He told the young man to do. The Bible says the young man was sad when Jesus asked him to get rid of his wealth. Now why do you think the man was sad? Why did he choose wealth over following Jesus? Well, it all goes back to: **Lay not up for yourselves treasures upon earth, where moth and rust do destroy and where thieves break in and steal: but lay up for yourselves treasures in heaven..., for where our trea-**

sure is, there your heart will be also. Or, as Paul writes in 1 Timothy 6:19, **Storing up for themselves a good foundation for the time to come, that they may lay hold on eternal life.**

This young man's treasure was his wealth — that was where his heart was. He did not want to give up his wealth, so he was sad when Jesus asked him to give it away. It was not because Jesus did not want the man to have things, but because He had perceived that the man was trusting in his riches.

What is being said, simply, is that what we do in this physical life should be first of all based upon what we do in the spirit world. When we do that, we will be operating in God's plan, in God's principles and in God's power. But if we allow ourselves to be taken up with this earthly life to the exclusion of the spirit world, then all we will do is reap all that the earth-realm can provide us with, and it can provide nothing that is lasting. Everything in the earth-realm is transitory and will pass away. But the things of the spirit will last forever. God wants us to get our treasure and our heart situated in the right place.

People talk negatively about me for talking about prosperity, but I have to do what God assigned me to do.

How many times have you ever heard Billy Graham preach on or teach on the subject of being filled with the Holy Spirit and speaking with other tongues? How many times have you ever heard him preach or teach on the subject of how to pray? Or on the subject of operating in the gifts of the Holy Spirit? What you have heard him preach on is salvation. The reason for that is because that is his assignment. And nobody has a problem with that.

I have listened to Billy Graham for more than 40 years. I began listening to him when I first got married and he was starting out in his evangelistic ministry. He has never changed his message. Basically, all he talks about is getting saved. Well, a part of my assignment is prosperity. And I cannot help but do what God directs me to do. Sometimes, I have plans to do other things and I find myself, just like an old wagon wheel, slipping right back into the rut.

The prosperity message is part of my assignment and part of the total package of knowledge that the Body of Christ needs. How often have you heard a minister talk about prosperity? It is a very neglected part of the Gospel. You almost have to be fanatical about it and go completely in the opposite extreme to get the old ship of Zion back on even keel like it ought to be.

Prosperity, like salvation and prayer, should have been taught in every Sunday school. But most people went through Sunday school and heard little if anything about prosperity or about being blessed going out and blessed coming in, or about having all their needs met or, being prosperous in this life spiritually, soulishly, physically and materially. Every Believer should have been taught about the importance of tithes and offerings in Sunday school, in catechism class, confirmation class, and all those other classes.

I heard a man talk about suffering as though it were something we were supposed to do. I had to squirm and sit there holding onto my seat, trying to be cool, calm and collected while he talked. God does not want you to suffer, and you don't find it in the Word. Such thinking is tradition, not God. Jesus suffered so we could be free.

1 Timothy 6:10:

For the love of money is a root of all kinds of evil, for which some have strayed from the faith in their greediness, and pierced themselves through with many sorrows.

That verse has been misquoted ever since the Bible was put into the language of the common people. It says, **For the love of money is a root of all kinds of evil....** Not money, but the love of it. You can love it and not have a dime in your pocket. That is why some folk are hitting other folk in the head to take what they have.

Now put that together with **trust not in uncertain riches....** And you will begin to see what the Father God wants to get across to us. He is not telling us to ignore money, because it takes money to run the Kingdom.

The Lord is speaking in Deuteronomy 8:18 to the children of Israel just prior to them going into the Promised Land when He says, **"And you shall remember the Lord your God, for it is He who gives you power to get wealth, that He may establish His covenant which He swore to your fathers, as it is this day."**

Remember, this is God Almighty talking. He gives *you* power to get the wealth, but *He* establishes the covenant. The reason you should have wealth is so that He may establish His covenant.

How does He establish His covenant? He establishes His covenant through His people. If we don't have the wealth, God cannot establish His covenant.

47

Salvation Is the Beginning

We have focused on one thing to the total neglect of all that Jesus came to do. John 10:10 says:

"The thief does not come except to steal, and to kill, and to destroy. I have come that they may have life, and that they may have it more abundantly."

Now that is what Christianity is all about.

Preachers need to read this because the Church has mistakenly thought that the only thing that God was interested in was getting folk saved. Sure, He is interested in getting folk saved, but getting saved for what? We have thought that salvation was missing hell when you die and going to heaven. That is all we thought Christianity was about — miss hell, go to heaven. So I get saved and I go to heaven. That is not what it is about at all. Salvation is a part of it, the New Birth is the *beginning,* but that is not the end.

I belonged to a Baptist church, a Methodist church, a Presbyterian church, and a Christian and Missionary Alliance church over a 17-year period, and all I ever heard in those churches was "get saved." They spent 17 years telling me to get what I already had 17 years before.

Nobody told me what to do with the salvation. Nobody told me what it was for. All they kept telling me every week was repent, repent, repent! Come to the altar, cry, shed tears, be sorry for your sins and confess the same ignorant dumb sin that I committed 12 years ago. They wanted me to confess it over and over and over again and, yet, never have any joy, any peace, and never be able to function on the very highest levels that God intended.

48

If that was all God wanted and if that is what it is all about, then the most natural thing to happen once you get saved is you ought to die, drop dead right then and go on to heaven. Jesus never said, I came that you might go to heaven. He said, "I came that you might have life...." Life!

1 Peter 3:10-11

> **For**
> **"He who would love life**
> **And see good days,**
> **Let him refrain his tongue from evil,**
> **And his lips from speaking deceit.**
> **Let him turn away from evil**
> **And do good;"**

Notice what these verses do not say. They do not say he who will love *heaven,* or love the sweet by-and-by, but love *life.*

If God your Father did not want you to have good days, then He would be working against himself by telling you how to have them.

God is saying that if you want to see good days, do these things. He did not say, if you want to suffer, do these things. He did not say, if you want to be afflicted all your days, do these things. He did not say, if you want to be in the hospital the rest of your life, do these things. He did not say, if you want to be poor the rest of your life, do these things; or if you wanted to be scared the rest of your life, do these things. He said that if you would love life and see good days, you should do these things.

God is saying that good days are not accidental. Good days are the result of your will. **He who would love life and see good days, let him refrain his tongue….**

It is up to you, not up to God. That is good news. It is a matter of your will. I can *will* to have good days. I can *will* to see good days. I can *will* to love life — and I love it! But I did not love it when I was sick; I did not love it when I was poor, and I did not love it when I could not meet my needs. I did not love it when I could not pay my bills, I did not love it when I watched my kids go without shoes. I did not love it in those days, but I love it now because every need is met. I love it now because I am blessed going out and I am blessed coming in. I am the head and not the tail. I am above and not beneath.

They did not tell me that in the Baptist, Methodist or any other church. They just said, "Hold on to God's unchanging hand. The Lord knows just how much you can bear."

I know a whole lot of folk who do not even believe in God, yet they have great lives, plenty of money, automobiles, plenty of all the world's goods. But friend, you are not with those people in the midnight hour. The world puts on a front.

Some people, before they came under the influence of Jesus Christ as their Savior and Lord, used to run the streets from sunrise to sunset. They seemed happy, but they were not. They were putting on a front. They would go home and cry the rest of the night. Everybody thought they were the life of the party. But they were not with them at two o'clock in the morning when those tears of loneliness came. Nobody can be complete without God in his or her life.

The world trusts in the uncertain riches. You take their riches from them and they have nothing left. That is why Matthew 6:33 is so important: **"But seek first the kingdom of God and His righteousness, and all these things shall be added to you."**

It says the things shall be *added*, not subtracted. First Timothy tells us that the *love* of money — not the money — causes you to lie, cheat, steal, connive, backbite and take another's life to get it. God does not want you to love money. He wants you to have it, but not to love it. Love Him and have the money, then He can direct you as to what to do with it and He can establish His covenant. We cannot establish God's covenant, but He can. However, He cannot do it without us because that is the way He has designed the system to work.

Mark 10:17-21:

> **Now as He was going out on the road, one came running, knelt before Him, and asked Him, "Good teacher, what shall I do that I may inherit eternal life?"**
>
> **So Jesus said to him, "Why do you call Me good? No one is good but One, that is, God.**
>
> **"You know the commandments: 'Do not commit adultery,' 'Do not murder,' 'Do not steal,' 'Do not bear false witness,' 'Do not defraud,' 'Honor your father and your mother.' "**
>
> **And he answered and said to Him, "Teacher, all these things I have kept from my youth."**
>
> **Then Jesus, looking at him, loved him, and said to him, "One thing you lack: Go your way, sell**

whatever you have and give to the poor, and you will have treasure in heaven; and come, take up the cross, and follow Me."

But he was sad at the word, and went away sorrowful, for he had great possessions.

Now this was an astute young man. He realized that he had to do something. Jesus told the man to sell everything — get rid of everything. That is awesome. Do you realize that would have left the man with no clothes on his back? It would have left him standing in the road stark naked? He would have had to give to the poor. The poor are not in heaven. The poor are on the earth, yet Jesus said when you do all of that, you will have treasure in heaven. The man would have treasure in heaven, but he was going to have to give his earthly possessions to poor folk on the earth. But when Jesus told him to give up his wealth to the poor, the man went away grieved and sad, **for he had great possessions.**

What's the spiritual truth to all of this? The main issue is, "Where is your heart?" The man had great possessions and the reasons he was blessed was because he was a doer of the Word. You might ask why would Jesus tell him to give his stuff away? Jesus was not interested in him giving anything away just for the sake of giving it away. That would be violating His Father's own law, because the Father had promised the Israelites in the 28th chapter of Deuteronomy that if they hearkened to His voice and observed to do all of His commandments, that they would be blessed going out and blessed coming in. He said their storehouses would be full.

Uncertain Riches

The Bible said the man had great possessions. But I absolutely believe that is a misquote. He did not have great possessions. *Great possessions had him,* and Jesus perceived that by the Spirit. Jesus perceived that the man was trusting in his possessions. And in order for him to have eternal life, he was going to have to cut himself loose from his present God in order to have the true and living God. And to prove to you how much those possessions had him, he could not turn them loose. The man came to Jesus and interrupted what Jesus was doing and asked him, "What shall I do?" Then, when Jesus told him, he went away sad. Why? Because great possessions had him. The love of money had him. He was trusting in the riches. The Bible proves it.

Look at Mark 10:23-24:

> **Then Jesus looked around and said to His disciples, "How hard it is for those who have riches to enter the kingdom of God!"**
> **And the disciples were astonished at His words.**

The disciples were astonished because usually in this earth-realm, the rich can have anything they want by virtue of their riches.

> **But Jesus answered again and said to them, "Children how hard it is for those who trust in riches to enter the kingdom of God!"**

Here was the man's problem — he trusted in the riches. But he was fine with everything else. The man's problem was his wealth. He had allowed the money to become his God and Jesus knew that he would never be able to enter the kingdom as long as he had that attitude. As a result,

53

Jesus set about separating him from his god (money), so that he could be free to enter the Kingdom. But Jesus did not want the man to be broke.

You might wonder why Jesus would tell the man to get rid of the wealth, for without the wealth, God would not be able to establish the covenant through the man. The only point of this Scripture was that Jesus perceived that the man was fixated on his wealth. He was trusting in those uncertain riches and Jesus wanted to cut him loose from them, but the man had to be willing to do it.

If God did not want you to have something, He could arrange the situation where you would lose it all. He could take it away from you through the circumstances. We, the children of God, can have the wealth and not trust in it. Instead, we must trust in the living God who provides the wealth.

We should understand that wealth is a tool, it is a servant. We can use our wealth to build a church sanctuary so that the people of God can gather under one roof and worship the Lord in spirit and in truth. That is how our dollars can serve us.

You can do a whole lot more if you have wealth than you can with a county welfare check.

Mark 10:25, 27:

"It is easier for a camel to go through the eye of a needle than for a rich man to enter into the kingdom of God."

... But Jesus looked at them and said, "With men it is impossible, but not with God; for with God all things are possible."

So if all things are possible, then a camel *can* go through the eye of a needle and a rich man *can* enter the Kingdom of God. He simply said, it is hard. And, remember that object lesson with the rich young ruler? It was hard for him. He could have entered the Kingdom if he willed to, but he didn't.

Once again, the reason that God does not want us to put our trust in uncertain riches is because they are subject to earthly conditions, so the earthly conditions will impact them and we will lose out.

We have found out several things:

1. We have a heavenly bank account, and Jesus encourages us to lay up for ourselves treasures in heaven where neither moth nor rust can corrupt and where thieves cannot break through and steal.

2. Jesus is not opposed to us having treasure; He just doesn't want us to put our hearts in the treasure.

3. Riches are not the problem, but trusting in them is the problem.

SIX

SALVATION — BASIS OF THE NEW COVENANT

What is the focal point of the New Covenant? It is salvation. The Scripture says it is not God's will that any perish. So, God's purpose in establishing His covenant is to bring salvation and redemption to mankind.

How does God get His plan of salvation to a dying world? How does He get out the message that He so loved the world that He gave His only son, or the message that Jesus died and rose again? What has God put into the earth-realm to bring this message of salvation to mankind? Anointed men and women, the Church, money, and television. He gave gifts unto men — apostles, prophets, evangelists, pastors, teachers — to perfect the saints. But how are the "ain'ts" going to become saints? They do that by accepting Christ as their personal Savior and Lord through the ministry gifts that work through the Church.

What is the covenant? The covenant is salvation. Because without salvation there is no redemption.

How is one to operate in the office of an apostle, prophet, evangelist, pastor and teacher and spend time telling the unsaved about salvation?

He has set those ministry gifts in the Church, and he did not tell them to work 40 hours a week. He did not tell them to go punch a clock. He said, "They that preach the Gospel should live of the Gospel." That means that those that God commissions to tell the "ain'ts" they can become saints, are supposed to be supported by the Gospel they preach and by the people to whom they minister.

I cannot work on a 40-hour-a-week job and effectively pastor my church. Teaching and pastoring is my job. So I put 40 hours a week into this line of work.

Now this is where the need for wealth comes in: it costs just as much for me to take care of my family as it does you to take care of your family. It costs just as much for me to buy shoes, a suit, and to fill my gas tank as it does for you. They do not give discounts on bread just because I am a minister. I have to pay property taxes, city taxes, income taxes, just like you do.

Where am I to get my money? How am I to be supported? The Bible says I should make my living by preaching. The wealth has to be available to supply the minister and his family with sustenance.

In order to tell the unsaved they can become saints I need to have the tools for my job. Most jobs have tools, equipment or uniforms intrinsic to their particular industry. It costs money to provide the tools to do a job. It costs money to be able to tell people about salvation. You need to have a facility to house the people so you can tell them about the Gospel. These are some of the reasons the Church needs wealth.

God's method of providing for His ministry gifts is not through chicken dinners or through barbecues. You do not find charcoal briquettes in the covenant. You do not find rummage sales in the Bible. So how are the men and women of God going to minister and be able to take care of their families? It will have to be through God's financial plan.

We at Crenshaw Christian Center had to build a church because there was no existing building that was large enough to seat our congregation, but the prospect of building a 10,000-seat auditorium was going to cost $12 million.

Our ministry is televised. We are attempting to reach people who would not be reached ordinarily by Christian television. As a rule, most non-Christians do not watch Christian television, so we have to get to them where they are — on secular television. That costs megabucks! Most Christians have tunnel vision and have no idea how much is spent to get the Gospel out. Television equipment — cameras, lenses, etc. — are very costly.

In the process of supporting the Gospel, all the supporters' needs will be taken care of. Not only their needs, but all their desires that are consistent with a godly life will also be supplied.

The New Covenant is about salvation, but it costs money to get salvation to the people. You do not have to pay to receive salvation; the product is free, but the pipeline to transport that Gospel is expensive.

God Wants to Save Rich and Poor

God loves people. We have had this idea in the church world that God only likes or loves the underdog, the guy on the bottom, and that is what we focused on. We have concentrated on the poor, on the homeless. But who makes any effort to minister to the president of AT&T? Don't you think Jesus died for the president of AT&T, or the president of the Disney Corporation?

Think of what would happen if the president of Disney got converted and became a tither — he earns many millions in annual salary. Do you know how many television stations we could go on with this message of salvation, the message of freedom, the message of faith and healing, the message of deliverance and power, if we had tithers like that? Money is all that stands between us and reaching more people. We can get on thousands of television stations if we only have the money.

God is interested in everybody, including movie stars. Don't you think Jesus cares about Sylvester Stallone? But you have to be on par with people like that in order to reach them. How are you going to spread the Gospel to Sylvester Stallone, saying "Praise the Lord!" and asking him to donate to the church with a little barbecue dinner in your hands! Do you think you are going to influence somebody like that? You have to get up where they are in order to converse with them, to even have the opportunity to rub shoulders with them. You need something in common even to get in the dressing room with them to talk about Jesus.

The average Christian will never get close to any of these people of influence. And no doubt about it, whether you like them or not, some of these wealthy and famous people do have great influence. They determine what we watch on television and what we see in the movies. What if every movie star got converted overnight? What would happen to the movie industry? Christians do not think about that sort of thing. They just think about their own selfish little concerns, such as selling more barbecue dinners, or more Katydid candies and holding more rummage sales.

Christians must begin to realize that our Father God sees the big picture, and that picture includes all mankind. He desires that none should perish.

But because the Christian community is so narrow-minded, they often find themselves stuck in misconceptions about the Father as well as the poverty-thinking syndrome, to the point of being in bondage to it.

We need to be able to give into the Gospel. The sinners are not going to support the Gospel; the Christians have to support it. In the process of God establishing His covenant through what we give, all our own personal needs and desires will be taken care of.

Many Christians are living substandard lives relative to wages. They are barely making it, and they do not know how to operate in the faith of God. They are suckers for the system, and most of them are just as much in debt as the sinners, living up to every nickel and dime they make. They can hardly give anything because they are in bondage.

I was in just as much bondage to debt. It was as bad as being an alcoholic or a drug addict. I would pass a store and see something that I just had to have. I was like somebody on drugs. The clerks would say, "Sign here, Mr. Price, and you will have no payment for 45 days." Those days passed so fast, it seemed as if the next day was the 45th day!

Some people are credit-card junkies and are just as bad as junkies on drugs. They do not know how to control their spending. They are in bondage — spend, spend, spend! Some people want to tithe, but they cannot afford to.

Thank God for His financial plan. He taught me how to get out of that mess, that bottomless pit, and still be able to have what I need and desire for myself and my family. Jesus said in John 10:10:

"I have come that they may have life, and that they may have it more abundantly."

Jesus wants you to have the desires of your heart. He tells us in Mark 11:24:

"... whatever things you ask when you pray, believe that you receive them, and you will have them."

You do not have to run drugs in order to get rich. You want to get a Mercedes-Benz — one that is all cut down and polished with the spoilers running around the bottom of it, the front of the thing all painted white, looking good? You can be a Christian and drive your Mercedes. You do not have to peddle drugs to do that.

It is not about Mercedes cars; I want you to understand that, so do not accuse me of being mercenary. But these are the kinds of things that are seducing our young people. And if they do not go to the church and find out how to get these things, they are going to find it out there on the street corner, in the gangs and with the drug pushers.

Our young people ought to find out they can be Christians with a clean life and clean heart and mind and still succeed financially as well as spiritually. And where should they be able to find it out? In the Church. But instead of God's ministers telling the children and young people they can have those things here on earth, they are telling them they are going to have to wait until they get to heaven.

Meanwhile, the drug pusher is standing outside the school every day telling the kid, "Look at that Mercedes. You want one like that? Here, I got a little something for you."

Our kids should know that they can serve Jesus Christ and drive a Rolls-Royce. This is what the majority of people are working for — not working to survive, they are working to satisfy their desires. And there is nothing wrong with that unless it becomes a substitute for seeking the Kingdom.

Don't let anybody con you — preachers or anybody else. You should seek Jesus, the Kingdom, first.

Thank God I can give now to support the Gospel because I learned how to operate in God's financial plan. Operating in His plan is how we were able to build the FaithDome. People tried to discourage us and say it could not be done; nobody could do it, but we did it — we and God. God and us — in the ghetto.

Our church is not located in suburban Los Angeles; it is in the ghetto. Nothing but crime is reportedly going on in the ghetto — rape, robbery, muggings, drugs, and murder. Nothing but bad news in the ghetto. But I have some good news for you, Jesus is going on in the ghetto and salvation is going on in the ghetto.

The Lord showed me that everything that has to do with the Gospel costs money. He told me He wanted me to have wealth so that He can get His covenant established — so that the "ain'ts" can become saints. He showed me that you can reach more people with wealth, under the direction and guidance of the Holy Spirit, than you can in poverty.

People do not have to be on welfare. Thank God for welfare, but some people are second- and third-generation welfare recipients.

Do not ever let anyone tell you that God is not interested in mankind. If He can find the people — a person, a group of people — who are willing, God will raise up a garden of Eden right in the middle of the desert. He will make it blossom like the rose of Sharon.

DEALING WITH MAN ON A PROGRESSIVE BASIS

The Lord's Prayer and the 23rd Psalm are probably the two most quoted passages in world literature. The 23rd Psalm is found in what is called the Old Testament, so when people read it, they have a tendency to think of it only in that context — something nice and beautiful, but under the Old Covenant.

But God has only one time to speak to men. The only time that God can speak to men is in the context of human history. The 23rd Psalm is a part of human history.

God deals with man on a progressive basis — He does not necessarily do everything at one time. He started out with Adam, then with a man named Abraham. He continued dealing with man through Abraham's son, Isaac, then Jacob and Jacob's 12 kids, then the nation of Israel, down to the age of the Church.

He revealed himself through human history, through the nation of Israel, and through the Bible on a progressive-revelation basis. Some truths that God reveals have limited application.

What I mean is that the truth revealed is only for a specific time in human history. For example, animal sacrifices under the Old Covenant were temporary — limited to that period of human history to expiate for man's sins. We do not sacrifice animals today. Jesus became the Lamb of God 2,000 years ago, so nobody has to sacrifice a turtledove or a lamb or a bullock or any other animal.

Some truths, however, have universal application. This truth is good for Old Covenant and New Covenant, for the beginning of human history, and the end of human history. It is not limited simply to one particular period, as animal sacrifices were. Here is an illustration: Psalm 91:1-7 says:

> **He who dwells in the secret place of the Most High**
> **Shall abide under the shadow of the Almighty.**
> **I will say of the LORD, "He is my refuge and my fortress;**
> **My God, in Him I will trust."**
>
> **Surely He shall deliver you from the snare of the fowler**
> **And from the perilous pestilence.**
> **He shall cover you with His feathers,**
> **And under His wings you shall take refuge;**
> **His truth shall be your shield and buckler.**
> **You shall not be afraid of the terror by night,**

Nor of the arrow that flies by day,
Nor of the pestilence that walks in darkness,
Nor of the destruction that lays waste at noonday.

A thousand may fall at your side,
And ten thousand to your right hand;
But it shall not come near you.

Later on, in Verse 16, He says, **"With long life I will satisfy him, and show him My salvation."**

The 91st Psalm has universal application. And it will work anytime, anywhere a man is willing to dwell in the secret place of the Most High. He has a right to that type of protection.

On the other hand, the Ten Commandments had limited application. It was only for a certain period of human history, after which it did not apply anymore.

The Law Is Not for Christians

Some of you might fall out with me regarding what I am about to say on this matter of the Ten Commandments, but I am just telling you what the Word of God says — not what tradition, a denomination or theology says.

The Ten Commandments do not work today. They are not for the Church of the Lord Jesus Christ. They were only for Israel. They are a part of the Law. The Law was not and is not for Christians. There are only two commandments under the New Covenant: to love the Lord your God with all your heart, with all your mind, with all your soul, with all your might, with all your strength, etc. That is the first commandment. The second is to love your neighbor as yourself.

God does not have to tell me, thou shalt not steal. Because if I love you, I will never steal from you. Love is a higher law than not stealing. There are man's laws that say do not steal and folk will steal from you anyway. But if I love you, I would never steal from you, I would never bear false witness against you.

Under the Old Covenant, the people were spiritually dead men. They had no capacity to operate in the agape or God-kind of love. They could not love one another with the love of the Lord. They could only love one another with a human kind of love and a human kind of love goes only so far: "If it is convenient, I love you. If you are pretty, I love you. If you do everything I want, I love you. But if you are homely and an ugly duckling, I do not love you." Face it; that is the truth. That is the way we operate in natural human life.

My purpose is not just to rock a lot of boats with what I teach. My purpose is to impart the truth. Jesus said the truth will make you free. I don't just say things to say them. I have an obligation here — when I say the Ten Commandments are not for us. I know multiplied thousands of people all over the world are still quoting or attempting to use what is called the Ten Commandments. You cannot separate the Ten Commandments from the Law, but they are only an infinitesimal part of the Law. If you break anything in the Law, you have broken the Law.

If you are going to lift the Ten Commandments out and use them, then you have to lift the animal sacrifices out and use them as well, because it is all a part of the Law.

1 Timothy 1:8-11:

> **But we know that the law is good if one uses it lawfully,**
>
> **knowing this: that the law is not made for a righteous person, but for the lawless and insubordinate, for the ungodly and for sinners, for the unholy and profane, for murderers of fathers and murderers of mothers, for manslayers,**
>
> **for fornicators, for sodomites, for kidnappers, for liars, for perjurers, and if there is any other thing that is contrary to sound doctrine,**
>
> **according to the glorious gospel of the blessed God which was committed to my trust.**

Christians do not need the Ten Commandments. God deals with us through our conscience, which has been quickened by the New Birth. God's purpose is to set men free.

Righteous or Holy?

If you ask the average Christian if they are righteous, whether they are Baptists, Presbyterians, Catholics, Methodists, Church of God in Christ or whatever else, most will not know what you are talking about. They do not know what righteousness is.

When I went to the Baptist church they never told me what it was. All they told me was about wearing certain kinds of clothes to show you are righteous. If you do not understand that you are righteous, then you will be hung up on this business about the Law.

First Timothy says, **knowing this, that the law is not made for a righteous person.**

Now you might not be very holy, but you are righteous. That's where the church world has misled Christians. They have amalgamated these two words — *holy* and *righteous* — and have become confused about their actual meanings.

Righteousness is one thing and holiness is something else. You might not be very holy, but you are righteous if you are born again. Holiness is something you do. Righteousness is something God does.

Romans 5:17 says:

For if by one man's offense death reigned through the one, much more those who receive abundance of grace and of the gift of righteousness will reign in life through the One, Jesus Christ.

A gift is something that is given just because the giver wants to give it. You cannot earn it. Otherwise, it is not a gift.

Romans 5:18-19:

Therefore, as through one man's offense judgment came to all men, resulting in condemnation, even so through one Man's righteous act the free gift came to all men, resulting in justification of life.

For as by one man's disobedience many were made sinners, so also by one Man's obedience many will be made righteous.

2 Corinthians 5:17-21:

Therefore, if anyone is in Christ, he is a new creation; old things have passed away; behold, all things have become new.

Now all things are of God, who has reconciled us to Himself through Jesus Christ, and has given us the ministry of reconciliation,

that is, that God was in Christ reconciling the world to Himself, not imputing their trespasses to them, and has committed to us the word of reconciliation.

Now then, we are ambassadors for Christ, as though God were pleading through us; we implore you on Christ's behalf, be reconciled to God.

For He made Him who knew no sin to be sin for us, that we might become the righteousness of God in Him.

Let me paraphrase the last verse: "For God made Christ who knew no sin to be sin for Fred, that Fred might become the righteousness of God in Christ."

Can you see that? Therefore, I am a righteous man. And so are you if you are a child of God.

From all that we talked about, you should now know that the Ten Commandments cannot be for Christians, because Christians are righteous. Righteousness is something God does for us. Holiness is our response through our lives, based on what God has done for us through Christ. Holiness has to do with the quality of our life. Righteousness

71

has to do with the place that we have in God because of Jesus. If you are not righteous, you are not saved.

We are made righteous, which simply means that we have right standing with God. Therefore, we have a right to come to God and expect that God will hear us when we approach Him through prayer.

EIGHT

CHRISTIANS' BILL OF RIGHTS

The New Covenant is the bill of rights for the Christian life, or literally the bill of righteousness.

Let's see how many people will want to be a part of the Law after reading this:

1 Timothy 1:9-10:

> Knowing this: that the law is not made for a righteous person, but for the lawless and insubordinate, for the ungodly and for sinners, for the unholy and profane, for murderers of fathers and murderers of mothers, for manslayers,
>
> for fornicators, for sodomites, for kidnappers, for liars, for perjurers, and if there is any other thing that is contrary to sound doctrine.

That is who the Law was made for, not for Christians.
If you disagree, it is the Bible you are disagreeing with, not
me, because I did not write it.

The 23rd Psalm is found in the Old Covenant, but I am
going to show you that it is a New Covenant principle. It is
not something simply to be quoted, it is something to live by.

In John 10:14, Jesus said:

**"I am the good shepherd; and I know My sheep,
and am known by my own."**

Psalm 23 is a New Covenant principle because in order
for the Lord to be your shepherd, you have to first be one of
His sheep. And you cannot be one of the sheep unless you
have been born again.

> **The LORD is my shepherd;**
> **I shall not want.**
> **He makes me to lie down in green pastures;**
> **He leads me beside the still waters.**
> **He restores my soul;**
> **He leads me in the paths of righteousness**
> **For His name's sake.**
>
> **Yea, though I walk through the valley of the
> shadow of death,**
> **I will fear no evil;**
> **For You are with me;**
> **Your rod and Your staff, they comfort me.**
>
> **You prepare a table before me in the presence
> of my enemies;**
> **You anoint my head with oil;**

My cup runs over.
Surely goodness and mercy shall follow me
All the days of my life;
And I will dwell in the house of the LORD
Forever.

The 23rd Psalm relates to all we have discussed before regarding prosperity, the Lord providing all of our needs, and treasure in heaven.

If God is your shepherd and you are His sheep and you are living in line with His covenant, you should never be in want. But something is wrong, because we have too many Christians who are in want.

The psalmist did not say that he did not want; he said, **The Lord is my shepherd; I shall not want**. But you will want if you do not know how to operate by faith in the covenant to take advantage of what God has provided for you. Because you have an enemy that will steal everything from you.

Multitudes of Christians are in want. I was in want for years, yet I was quoting Psalm 23. And while I was quoting it, they were cutting the lights off because I could not pay the bill. Either God lied or I did not know what I was supposed to be doing and what I was about.

I am a living witness that when you learn how to walk by the Word and by faith, you will get to a point in life where you will not be in want. I could not always say that. Right now I do not have one unmet need in my life, not one that I cannot go and meet right this second. When I first started out as a Christian, I had none of my needs met, so I never even got into desires or wants. I have lots of desires that I am working on now, but I do not have a need for anything. Even if it is not in manifestation, I have the resources to meet it.

When people hear me say such things, they say things like, "That's why I ain't giving him any money, 'cause he's talking about he ain't got no needs."

Let me ask you this question: Do you give to God because He is in need? The answer is no. You give to Him because you love Him. You ought to be giving to me because you love me, not because I have a need.

The Lord is my shepherd, I shall not want, because I found out how to walk in His covenant. And God wants me to share it with you. God wants you to be able to say the same thing, live in the same situation and the same privilege. These privileges in Christ are not just for me, they are for the entire Body of Christ.

That second verse of the 23rd Psalm proves that God is not the one bringing all these calamities on people. Hurricanes, typhoons, tornadoes, earthquakes and such are called "acts of God" by the world. But the Bible said God leads me beside still waters — not raging, turbulent waters, but still waters — where you can cross in safety, where you can swim till your heart's content.

The psalmist says God **leads me besides the still waters**. When the waters are quiet, you can wade in them and not have to be concerned about being inundated by the flood.

So, if your life is circumscribed by boisterous waves, by howling winds, then you know you are not being led by the Lord, because the Word says He leads you by still waters. The questions are, "Are you listening?" and "Are you following?" Maybe the reason the storm is going on in your life is because you are not following.

He restores my soul.... This is talking about salvation. I learn as much by what the Word does not say as by what it does say. When you restore something you put it back the way it was. If that is so, you are working with the same thing you started out with, not something new. Notice it does not say He restores my *spirit*, nor restores my *life*. It says, **He restores my soul.**

Your soul is your personality. It contains your desire, your will, your emotions, your human intellect. The soul is what makes you you and me me.

When you are born again, that implies brand-new life, a spiritual birth. This is supported by 2 Corinthians 5:17, which says:

> **Therefore, if anyone is in Christ, he is a new creation.**

New creation means one that never was before. That is not talking about restoration.

The biggest challenges we have in my church, Crenshaw Christian Center, is dealing with people's souls. The challenges we have to face are all soulish in nature, because souls are in rebellion. They want their way, and, if they do not get their way, they cry, whine, complain, gripe, grumble and sow seeds of discord. All of that is in the soul-realm and the soul has to be restored. That restoration takes time.

All of this has to do with God's financial plan, because if you do not have a basic understanding of spiritual matters, you will never be able to operate to the fullest in the plan. Your head will get in the way. Your soul will mess you up.

HIGHER FINANCE

James 1:21:

> **Therefore lay aside all filthiness and overflow of wickedness, and receive with meekness the implanted word, which is able to save your souls.**

James did not say it *would;* he said it is *able* to save your soul. Yet he is talking to saved people, born-again people. So the words *save your soul* must not mean what we usually take them to mean in common usage — getting born again. James is writing to born-again people.

What does he mean when he says **save your souls**? He is saying that God's Word will change your personality, your mind, your emotions, your intellect, your behavior. You can see why there are people who have become new creatures in Christ Jesus and have never done anything about their souls. Their personalities are just like they were before they got saved or born again. You can understand why Christians act so crazy and ugly, why they tell lies, why they fornicate, why they sow seeds of discord, why they act like little babies and you have to pat each one of them on the head individually or they get their feelings hurt. It is because their souls have not yet been saved.

One of the ways you know so many Christians are a work in progress is because so many are cheap-minded penny-pinchers.

There are Christians who don't tithe. They cannot bring themselves to give 10 percent. Yet, they go to a restaurant and give 15 percent to a perfect stranger and do not even blink an eye. In fact, they are proud to give that tip, they are the last of the big spenders in a restaurant. In church, however, they say, "I ain't gonna give no preacher none of my money." But they gave the waitress 15 percent and she did not even cook their food. All she did was deliver it from the kitchen to their table.

When you get your soul like it ought to be, you begin to think like God thinks. God thinks big. He thinks gigantic. He is not stingy. He is not a penny-pincher.

Romans 12:1-2:

I beseech you therefore, brethren, by the mercies of God, that you present your bodies a living sacrifice, holy, acceptable to God, which is your reasonable service.

And do not be conformed to this world, but be transformed by the renewing of your mind, that you may prove what is that good and acceptable and perfect will of God.

What God wants us to do is bring our minds in line with the mind of Christ so that we think like He thinks. The only way you will know how God thinks is by getting into His Word, which the Shepherd will use to restore your soul. The Shepherd has been restoring my mind because I was willing to be led. Every Christian ought to be led.

You cannot comprehend the greatness and goodness of God until you learn how to get your soul restored and your head screwed on right and get lined up with the things of God. If you do not get your mind-set changed to correspond to God's Word, you will never be able to operate in God's financial plan as you ought. You will still have a penny-pinching idea of life and of God and of the things of God.

As a result, you will be groveling in the dust, always in want and need because God cannot respond to a penny-pinching attitude.

I met a real penny-pincher one day when I went to get my car serviced. When this guy saw me driving a Rolls-Royce, he was astounded and told me he was going to tell his mother to cut back on her contributions to my ministry. In other words, he felt that because I was driving a Rolls-Royce, his mother should not be making financial contributions to me because I must already have enough money. But I told the guy it was none of his business what kind of car I drove — the car was a gift anyway, and his mother's contributions were going to the ministry to help change people's lives. Besides, I was ministering to her — not him — and obviously she was pleased with what she was getting from the ministry of God's Word. What difference did it make what kind of car I drove? And why shouldn't I drive a Rolls-Royce if I want to?

That is the kind of cheap thinking many people have — even Christians. It is perfectly okay if they see a person in the world driving the best kind of car, but God's people are not supposed to have the best.

If people stop giving to my ministry simply because they want to prevent me from driving a Rolls-Royce, they are in error.

I know folk who have been going to church for 25 years and they are just as mean, stingy, ornery and backbiting as they can be. They gossip and speak negatively about others all the time. Every time the church door flies open, they fly in! There is no change because their souls have not been restored.

Shadows Cannot Hurt You

That psalm also says, **Yea, though I walk through the valley of the shadow of death....**

It does not say, *Yea, though I walk through the valley of death*. It is telling us that death has no rightful claim on the sheep, and that when we walk through the valley, only the *shadow of death* can come upon us, unless we fail to allow the Shepherd to lead us.

You are not walking through a valley of death; he said the **valley of the shadow**. Nothing but the shadow is going to pass on you. And the shadow cannot hurt you.

Years ago, I went to a zoo. As we were passing animals in cages, I turned and saw my shadow and this form moving and bending over it. When I turned and looked up, I saw a cage with a huge boa constrictor — one that could swallow a young pig whole. I wiped the perspiration from my brow as I stood back and said, "Isn't that something! That snake cannot hurt me. Only the shadow passed over me." And when we walk through the valley of the shadow of death, it cannot hurt us.

Until I found out about my covenant and how to walk by faith, I was scared of dying. Fear had me, it gripped me. Once in a while I would find myself thinking about dying and I would be shaking because the thought of death brought fear with it. The reason death brings fear is because death is not from God.

I will fear no evil, says the 23rd Psalm. Why tell me about evil in relation to walking through the valley of the shadow of death? What does evil have to do with walking through the valley of the shadow of death? It is because death is evil. It is not of God. We can make the best out of a bad situation, yet death does not come from God.

Death was never in God's plan. You were not created to die. You were created to live. if you are walking around like I was — always afraid of dying, it is very difficult to enjoy God's financial plan.

1 Corinthians 15:26:

The last enemy that will be destroyed is death.

Death is an enemy, not a friend. But God said death will be destroyed, therefore death could not come from God, because then we would have to destroy God. Thank God that one of these days death will be destroyed.

If you are afraid of death, then you are not walking in your covenant rights, or perhaps you have never been born again — or you do not know about this. But if you know your covenant, you will know this information.

You need to underline the words *I will*. Why? Because your will is involved. If you are afraid, it is because you *will* to be afraid. The Bible says, **I will fear no evil.** It does not say evil will not make me afraid. It says, I will fear no evil. Fear is an act of your will.

IGNORANCE AND LACK

Hosea 4:6:

My people are destroyed for lack of knowledge.

G od's people are destroyed, not because they do not love Him enough, not because they do not go to church enough, not because they do not pray enough, or not because they do not give tithes and offerings. God said, **My people are destroyed for lack of knowledge.** One simple thing — knowledge. In other words, they are ignorant.

They are being destroyed, being eaten alive by Satan and his demon hordes just because they do not know who they are, what they have, what they can do, or what has already been done for them.

That is why the Lord told me to go on television. He told me to feed His sheep and to feed His lambs. He told me He no longer wanted His people destroyed for lack of knowledge. Now, that does not mean I have all the revelation in the Bible and know it all, but if you listen you will learn something from what I have to say.

God does not want His children destroyed for lack of knowledge. You cannot operate on what you do not know. You cannot claim what you do not know is yours, you cannot participate in something you do not know is there. You cannot take advantage of something that you do not know has been offered to you.

God told me to teach, don't preach. He said there was plenty of whooping and hollering. He said, no music. That does not mean we cannot, on some occasion, have something special. But all the years we have been on television, it has been basically just teaching, because that is what is going to help people in the midnight hour when they are alone wondering how they are going to cope. That will help you when the economic wolf comes knocking at your door — knowledge about who you are, knowledge about what you can do, and knowledge about what you have in Christ.

It is not enough just to say, "Praise the Lord, hallelujah." We ought to do that at the appropriate time, of course, but when it gets down to the nitty-gritty, you better know more than "praise the Lord." You had better know what thus *saith* the Lord.

There are principles that govern God's financial plan. We need to know what they are so that we can cooperate with the plan and, of course, reap the benefits. If God did not want us to have the benefits, He never would have told us about them. So, to me, it is disobedience on my part if I do not walk in the fullness of God's covenant and provisions.

If I am afraid, I am afraid in disobedience to the Word of God because fear does not come from the Father. We have nothing to be afraid of.

I am glad that I found out that my Father is not my problem. He is not my enemy, but He is my friend.

Psalm 23 says, **Your rod and Your staff, they comfort me.**

God's rod, God's staff for us are His Word and His covenant and all of its benefits. This comforts me. I have comfort here in the Word of God. Why? Because I have God's will revealed to me. I know what God's will is for my life and so I do not have to be afraid of evil tidings. I have the rod and the staff. I can support myself, steady myself on God's Word and not be afraid of anything.

Psalm 23:5:

> **You prepare a table before me in the presence of my enemies.**

Many people have the idea that what is in this psalm is for some future date. But the 23rd Psalm is actually a New Covenant principle that can be fully appreciated and experienced only under the New Covenant, because it started out by saying, **The Lord is my shepherd.** Jesus is the shepherd. He said, **"I am the good shepherd"** and we are the sheep.

We are the ones who can really experience the full benefit. David experienced some of it as he walked with God under the Old Covenant, but it is only under the New Covenant that we fully get into the benefits of Psalm 23.

Psalm 23 is not for over there on the other side. **In the presence of my enemies,** which means in front of them — right in the face of the enemies. That could not be talking about when we are in heaven because there are no enemies in heaven. The benefits of Psalm 23 have to be in this life-time. It has to be now, while we are living here, because this is the only place where we have enemies.

Isn't it interesting that He says He will do it in the pres-ence of my enemies? Don't you know that will goad the enemies? Don't you know that is like putting salt on the wound? And there won't be a thing in the world the en-emies can do about it, unless you let them.

You anoint my head with oil. That is a symbol of the Holy Spirit. The Holy Spirit was not given under the Old Covenant, but He is under the New Covenant. Every born-again Believer can be a partaker of the Holy Spirit. He is a gift that has been given to the Body of Christ.

The latter part of that verse says, **My cup runs over.** Do you know what happens when something runs over? That means there is an abundance, there is more than enough. That is divine provision, divine supply. That is not living on Barely-Get-Along Street, way down the block next to Grumble Alley.

Why do you suppose your cup runs over? The reason it runs over is so you will have some to share with those who do not have it yet. If you have more than enough, that means you have enough to share with others. That is when the fun begins. That is when it gets to be joy unspeakable and full of glory — when you can move out of thinking about just meeting your need and start becoming a channel of blessing to meet the need of others.

He wants you to have more than enough. He doesn't want you to barely make ends meet — He wants them to overlap.

Now you will never get that level of abundant supply until you find out how to operate in God's financial plan. The devil, the circumstances and the world system that we live under will not allow you to have an abundant supply. But there is a way to do it and a place to do it in God through the covenant.

Jesus said, **... those things he says will be done, he will have whatever he says.**

I started saying that more than 20 years ago, even when my cup did not even have a bottom in it. There was nothing but a handle and something around it that the handle was attached to. It did not have a bottom, let alone anything in it.

But I started saying, "My cup runs over, my cup runs over," and as I began hearing myself saying that, another law started working — **So then faith comes by hearing, and hearing by the word of God.** I started saying it, and I would look in the cupboard, so to speak, and see it with my eye of faith, and I began calling those things which be not as though they were.

I kept saying it, even though I know people thought I was strange. But it did not bother me. Folk have thought worse things. I was operating in the covenant. I had God's Word.

Either my cup runs over or God lied to me. The Bible said it is impossible for Him to lie, so I kept on saying it, "My cup runs over." I know some people said, "Now look at that fool, talking about his cup runs over. Isn't he crazy." Crazy like a fox.

God wants me to share this with you to inspire and encourage you. There was a time when I could not put five dollars in a Sunday-morning offering. But now, on any given Sunday, I put in several thousand dollars.

I can look the economic lion in the eye today and tell him, "Get back, lion!"

Thank God for heaven, but heaven will take care of itself. God wants you to prosper in *this* life.

Material things are not what it is all about, but they will get people's attention, and before you can ever help a person, you have to get their attention. You have to deal with them where they are.

Jesus said at one time, **"Be wise as serpents, but harmless as doves."** Wisdom dictates a method is needed to reach the wealthy person. And the Church has never thought about that; they think about reaching poor sinners, but they limit who sinners are. They have their own idea about who sinners are.

Sinners are everywhere. And you will never reach some of the big executives by selling chicken dinners to raise money to keep the church doors open. That will never get their attention.

Jesus reached people on every stratum, and the reason He did is because He was able to relate to everybody. When they began talking about finances, he pulled money out of a fish's mouth. When they started talking about supply and demand, He would take a loaf of bread and multiply it and feed 5,000 men plus the women and children.

When the sick came, He treated them. He got the medical society of that time interested in what He was doing. If you can reach the guy on the top rung, you can reach everybody below. But if all you can do is reach the guy in the gutter, you will never get the guy in those ivory towers or those high-rise office buildings across the nation.

God wants to reach everyone, but He can only do it through us. We are the ambassadors for Christ. What does an ambassador do? He represents his country.

There are tragic conditions in society. If you think about all the homeless and hungry people, you have to realize that there are people elsewhere eating pheasant under glass every night. They have private cooks who prepare them the kind of things you hardly see in the finest restaurants in our nation. Some people eat like that every day, while other folk are starving outside their gates. They are living what we call "high on the hog." So you can see that there can be abundance in the midst of lack and want.

The Level of Abundance

God wants to bring every person who is willing up to that same level. There are no shortages of supplies. All shortages are manufactured shortages or psychological shortages so that prices can be driven up and the rich can get richer. There is plenty of everything. In fact, they throw away more stuff than we will ever use. They throw away more food than you can ever buy.

God wants every person who is not His child to become His child. And he wants His children to be abundantly supplied. He built a world and stocked it with everything that is necessary for everybody to be abundantly supplied, but we have an enemy who does not want us to take advantage of it.

God has a plan and the Lord wants me, as a minister of the Gospel, to tell you about it.

Psalm 23:6:

Surely goodness and mercy shall follow me....

God does not say goodness and mercy shall follow me. He does not say "maybe," "could be," "might be," "it's possible," "could happen." No! He says "surely" goodness and mercy shall follow me all the days of my life. Do you realize the magnitude of that statement? He says "surely" goodness, not badness, will follow me.

If you watch this very carefully, you will see the discrepancy between traditional religion, theology, and denominationalism throughout the years. They tell us that all the bad in the world is from God. They say, "The Lawd did it." But the Bible says "surely goodness" — not badness, not sickness, not disease, not poverty, not fear. Not only goodness, but "goodness and mercy." It does not say that goodness and mercy will be somewhere in your state. It does not say that goodness and mercy will probably appear somewhere in your neighborhood. Surely goodness and mercy shall "follow me." So as you are walking down the path of life, look behind you and see goodness and mercy. Not badness and judgment, but goodness and mercy!

Let me stop right here and clarify this statement. Remember that this does not work unless you work it. This will not function unless you do your part. There are two sides to this — there is the man side, and there is the God side.

You do not have to worry about God doing His part. He will do His part, but His part can only be initiated and activated by us doing our part. That is why He gave us the Bible and that is why He told us about His plan, so that we would know how to cooperate with Him to release His goodness and mercy to follow us. They are not going to follow us if we are going into a whorehouse! Goodness and mercy are going to stop at the curb.

There are conditions; it just doesn't work arbitrarily. The condition is that the Lord is our shepherd — that presupposes that we are His sheep. And if we are the sheep, then we ought to act like a sheep and not like goats. And some Christians have been acting like goats — stubborn, mean, unreliable — half-stepping with the things of God. You ought to start acting like sheep. Read your covenant and it will tell you the rules and regulations about sheeping.

If you are doing your part, then goodness and mercy will follow you, not run off and leave you, but follow you. It does not say surely goodness and mercy shall follow you in good times. It does not say goodness and mercy shall follow you during leap year. It does not say goodness and mercy shall follow you during the summer solstice of the vernal equinox. It says goodness and mercy shall follow you all the days of your life.

You are supposed to have it good all the days of your life. And you will, if you follow the covenant. The covenant is more than just coming to church. It is more than just showing up with a notebook and a pen to take notes. It is more than marking Scriptures with a yellow highlighter.

God wants you to prosper and live the abundant life, but you have to do it His way.

Psalm 23:6:

And I will dwell in the house of the LORD Forever.

Now I believe that Psalm 23 proves very clearly, along with the other Scriptures, that God wants me to prosper. Based on that, let us get into the mechanics of God's financial plan. How does it actually work?

TEN

How God's Financial Plan Works

I know how to make a deposit in my local bank. I get a deposit ticket, which has my account number on it. I fill it out, put the date on it and take it to the bank with my passbook to deposit in the bank. When they credit it to my account, I can write checks on it out of my checking account.

How do we make deposits in the Kingdom of God? In this chapter, I want to deal with two things I positively, unequivocally know will produce results for you. But let me first share how I began to understand God's financial plan.

When God called me to the ministry, I heard what I believe was an audible voice — that is how real it was to me more than 40 years ago. I did not see any lights like Paul did on the road to Damascus, but I heard a voice loud and clear. Nobody else in the building heard the voice, but I heard it, loud, like a trumpet sound, "You are to preach my Gospel."

But when God called me and anointed me for the ministry, I was in lack. Over a 17-year period, I preached the Gospel and I had a cup with no bottom in it. In fact, after 17 years, the cup was sitting, levitating in space because the cupboard had fallen apart by that time. I did not even have a cupboard then. I was a minister and still my cup was empty.

It was not until I found out about these principles I am sharing with you, and began to operate in them that my life began to change. I became aware that some construction work was going on in the kitchen of my life, so to speak, and the power of God was starting to build cabinets in my cupboard.

Then very shortly after that, I started seeing little specks of stuff in the bottom of the cup. At first I thought it was dirt, but after a closer examination, I found out it was the blessings of the Lord. And those blessings just kept on rising in the cup, getting bigger and bigger. Finally, the blessings started running out over the brim of the cup. It got so good until they started running out of the cupboard onto the countertop. I did not know what I was going to do because I thought we were going to be flooded! And then they ran out on the floor, and out of the back door, into the garage, and then they were *everywhere!*

But the blessings did not start there. They did not start out running everywhere. I started out with a bottomless cup on a shelfless cupboard, but I stayed with it.

This metaphoric scenario illustrates just how God's Word and blessings began to work in my life. And since God is no respecter of persons, His word and financial plan can work in your life as well.

God's Word does not work because I am a preacher, and His blessings won't overtake you because you are a minister. I can show you ministers all over this country who are poor. They don't have a pot to cook in.

How do we make a deposit in our heavenly bank account?

I have never yet had anyone make a deposit in my worldly checking account unbeknownst to me. Have you? In other words, I have not gone to the bank and had the banker say, "Mr. Price, you have a million dollars in the bank. Somebody just deposited a million dollars for you!" In fact, I have not had anyone deposit even one dollar for me. All the money that ever went into my checking account, I deposited, or my wife deposited on my behalf. Nobody on the outside made those deposits. I say that to say this: Jesus said, "**... lay up for yourselves treasures in heaven.**" If *you* do not lay them up, guess what? There will be none laid up for you!

People have this fanciful idea that the Lord will do it. No! The man told you to lay it up, he did not say the Lord would. That means that is my responsibility; plus, it means I can. If He told me to do it, then I am capable of doing it. Let us find out how we do it.

There is no point in the preacher telling you to "**lay up for yourselves treasures in heaven,**" and not telling you how to do it. I am willing to obey God — and you probably are too — if you can find out how to do it.

There *is* a way, and the Bible tells us exactly how to do it. There are two primary ways — there might be other ways, but I found two that are working so well for me, I don't need the third and the fourth and the fifth ways.

The first way is tithing; the second way is investing in the Gospel.

I want to be very clearly understood — and I know a lot of people do not understand it because many people write me notes and sometimes they will say, "I wanted to pay my t-i-d-e-s." They think that we are saying *tides*, like the ocean is coming in. I want you to understand what we are talking about.

Look at Malachi 3:8-12:

> **"Will a man rob God?**
> **Yet you have robbed Me!**
> **But you say,**
> **'In what way have we robbed You?'**
> **In tithes and offerings.**
> **You are cursed with a curse,**
> **For you have robbed Me,**
> **Even this whole nation.**
> **Bring all the tithes into the storehouse,**
> **That there may be food in My house,**
> **And try Me now in this,"**
> **Says the LORD of hosts,**
> **"If I will not open for you the windows of**
> **heaven**
> **And pour out for you such blessing**
> **That there will not be room enough to receive it.**
>
> **"And I will rebuke the devourer for your sakes,**
> **So that he will not destroy the fruit of your**
> **ground,**
> **Nor shall the vine fail to bear fruit for you in**
> **the field,"**

> Says the LORD of hosts;
> "And all nations will call you blessed,
> For you will be a delightful land,"
> Says the LORD of hosts.

Some of you would say, "We're under the New Covenant and Malachi is in the Old Testament. We're under grace, not under the Law, and as a result of that, we don't have to tithe."

Well you are right about the last thing — you don't *have* to tithe. But you had better if you do not want to be arrested for robbing God.

Even though I touched on this in an earlier chapter, I want to reiterate it, so that you will keep firmly in your mind the idea that tithing is for us today. It is one of God's principles that has universal application.

Tithing was one of the things that God said to man. When God asks us to do something, it is not for His benefit, it is for ours. He is God whether we do what He says or not. He was God before we came into existence, so He does not need anything we have to maintain His godliness. He is God without us. If He tells us to do something, He must have a reason.

He told us to bring all the tithes into the storehouse.

He says the whole nation is cursed with a curse because they have robbed Him.

At the time God said this, He was talking to Israel, because Israel was His only contact point with humankind at that time. He started out with Adam. Adam messed up, short-circuited the system, and God had to circumvent the system and find another obedient man. First it was Abram, and then

Isaac, and Jacob, and then came the twelve tribes of Israel. He dealt with mankind in general through the nation of Israel. They were His channel. He was talking to Israel at the time, but we also are a nation or a kingdom of priests. Under the New Covenant, we are a holy people, a peculiar people. And we are a royal priesthood. So God is still dealing with the world through His representatives under this dispensation, which is the Church of the Lord Jesus Christ — *church*, meaning those who have been born again. God works through the Body of Christ to reach the world through His Son, Jesus Christ.

Notice what He said to Israel. He said, **"You are cursed with a curse, for you have robbed Me ... bring all the tithes into the storehouse."**

Now isn't that an interesting statement? God said bring all the tithes. He knew that some of the people would try to hold out on some of the tithes, but He said to bring *all* the tithes.

Didn't we read about laying up for ourselves treasures in heaven? And God said, **bring all the tithes**, so that is one of the ways you make deposits in heaven. He also said He would open **the windows of heaven and pour out for you such blessing....** We are always the recipients, the ones who benefit when we give.

Now why does God ask us to tithe? Because He wants to bless us. Tithing is for our benefit, not God's. And yet, He has arranged it so that we would not be tempted to steal from ourselves. Even though He says, **"Will a man rob God?"** actually you are not robbing God, you are robbing yourself. How are you going to take something away from God? Nevertheless, He says if you do not tithe you rob Him. So what God does is take up our cause. Isn't that beautiful?

He said he would **"open for you the windows of heaven and pour out for you such blessing that there will not be room enough to receive it."** So tithing is for our benefit, not for God's.

I was watching a man coming to church one Sunday, smoking a cigarette. Thank God he stopped smoking before he got on the grounds, but by smoking that cigarette, he was stealing from himself. People do it all the time, steal from their wives, their husbands, children, their parents. Man is a habitual thief, and if you don't watch him, he will steal. And God, because He knows his children, designed the system of tithing to help us toe the line.

God wants me to be blessed not cursed.

Verse 8 says you are **cursed with a curse.**

Why? Because you have robbed God. Actually, you are cursed because you robbed yourself, and there are a lot of people who are cursed financially and wonder why they have such a hard time in life. It is because they are cursed because they are robbing God.

Tithing is a universal concept that God intends every one of his creatures to participate in. God wants you blessed. That is why He made this great big beautiful earth. Do you realize that God could have made a barren globe? If He is God, He is smart enough to figure out how to make things work without all of the things that He has on earth. Don't think God is just locked into one way. He made it like that, but He made it for our benefit and our enjoyment. He can make anything He wants to make as long as it conforms to His own purpose and plan.

Tithing Practiced Before the Law

Tithing was in operation 430 years before the Law was even given. It did not originate with the Law. It was placed in the context of the Law so that people under the Law could be blessed, because God wants His creatures blessed, not cursed.

The Old Testament is not the Law of God, or what is usually referred to as "the Law." The Law is contained within the Old Testament. In fact, only five of the 39 Old Testament books are actually the Law — Genesis, Exodus, Leviticus, Numbers and Deuteronomy. They are called the Pentateuch.

Jesus refers to what is called "the Law and the prophets." Whatever is not the prophets is the Law, and whatever is not the Law is the prophets — but they are different. The Law is not the whole Old Testament.

The Law was instituted at Mount Sinai by God through Moses. The man we are going to read about lived long before Moses.

Genesis 14:13-20:

... Then one who had escaped came and told Abram the Hebrew ... and they were allies with Abram. [Abram is later to become known as Abraham.]

Now when Abram heard that his brother was taken captive, he armed his three hundred and eighteen trained servants who were born in his own house, and went in pursuit....

100

> **He divided his forces against them by night,
> and he and his servants attacked them and pursued
> them as far as Hobah, which is north of Damascus.
> So he brought back all the goods, and also
> brought back his brother Lot and his goods....
> Then Melchizedek king of Salem ...said:
> "... Blessed be Abram of God Most High,
> Who has delivered your enemies into
> your hand."
> And he gave him a tithe of all.**

The definition of tithe is tenth — one-tenth or ten per-cent. Abram gave this priest Melchizedek tithes. He must have known about the tithe in order to give it. Not only that, but this man Melchizedek must have known about tithes in order to receive it. Abram felt comfortable giving this man the tithe because he recognized that Melchizedek would know and understand what the tithe meant.

The Bible did not say he gave Melchizedek some money. It did not say he gave him some things, but **he gave him a tithe of all**. When it says a tithe of all, that means ten percent of gold, of silver, of cattle, of sheep, of anything. He gave him a tithe of all. So, whatever he had recovered in this battle, Abraham, or Abram, gave 10 percent of all of it.

Abram paid tithes, Melchizedek received tithes. There-fore, tithing must have been in force. In other words, tithing must have been a principle that people lived by or Abram would not have known to give a tithe.

Why would the Holy Spirit call it a tithe if it wasn't something that those who lived in that day would be able to relate to? Why not just say that Abram gave him some of everything that he recovered. Why use the term *tithe* unless it is to alert us to the fact that they paid tithes in those days.

Genesis 13:1-2:

Then Abram went up from Egypt, he and his wife and all that he had, and Lot with him, to the South.
Abraham was very rich in livestock, in silver, and in gold.

A lot of you have been working for years, you have been working your brains out and you still do not have anything and you are wondering what in the world is going on. You still are not making it, not like you would like to make it. Yet you are putting in the time.

This passage lets us know that Abraham had abundance, and he got it by being obedient. And who gave it to him? God.

God wants His people blessed. He wants them to be prosperous because He is prosperous and He wants them to enjoy that which He has created. He did not create it for Satan's children. He created it for His own children, but there is a way to get it that is right and legitimate, and there is a dishonest way. He does not want us to get trapped into the dishonest way, so tithing was incorporated into the Law so that the people under the Law could be blessed by God's financial plan.

Tithing has always been God's method of blessing His people. Genesis 13:1-2 tells how Abram was blessed.

God told Abram in Genesis 12:2:

"...I will bless you and make your name great;
And you shall be a blessing."

In the 13th chapter of Genesis, it says that Abram was very rich. God doesn't choose welfare recipients, as such, as role models for how He wants His children to behave. And He doesn't choose Skid Row bums or the homeless, necessarily.

I am not saying God is not concerned about these people, but I want to help you get away from the idea that you have to be poor in order to be a Christian. I want you to see that God is not impressed with poverty, though unfortunately, this is the mentality of the organized church world. The idea of poverty as kind of a status symbol for Christians has been promulgated down through the years.

God started out by using a man — Abraham — and then God made the man rich.

It does not say that Abraham had a lot of things. It does not say that Abraham was in good shape. It does not say that Abraham had a great financial statement. It says Abraham was *very* rich. Can you comprehend the term *rich*? Then look at the descriptive term *very rich*.

I realize that I may talk about this a lot, but it is part of my assignment. All God's ministers need to teach on this subject, but most have been fooled by the religious idea that you are not supposed to have anything. In fact, some ministers go so far as to take what they call a vow of poverty. In certain denominations that is what they call it. It is really a vow of ignorance — ignorance of God's Word. They mean well, they are sincere, but they are sincerely wrong.

Likewise, many Believers have made a grave mistake in the idea of poverty or riches in relationship to being a Christian.

In Genesis 24:34, you read about this servant in another land telling people about his master, Abram, and how the Lord has blessed Abram with cattle, and silver, etc. Now I ask a question: Who told the servant that the Lord had given the things to Abram? How did he know it was the Lord? We have no indication that he was a worshipper of Jehovah God. How did the servant know the Lord blessed his master, Abram?

He knew because Abraham told him. It seems like a simple thing, but it was a great revelation to me because it gave me more proof for the way God has had me to minister to my congregation about things that God has done in my life.

When I first started walking in faith, walking by the Word, and the Lord began to bless me, my wife and I started traveling. God began to call us to go to different places to minister. And when I would come back home and show my kids the honorariums, the checks that people gave me for ministering, I would say to them, "See, this is what the Lord did." They grew up knowing that everything that their mother and I had, God gave it to us. Why did I tell them? Because I wanted them to know you can serve God and prosper.

A lot of people have the idea that God and prosperity are diametrically opposed. This is the way tradition has led us to believe.

Some people have sold their souls in order to achieve in this world. You often have to do a lot of things out there in the world to be a success, like step on folk, pull deals, and do some things under the counter. In the world system, they make it hard for you to do what is right to succeed — even if you want to do what is right. You almost have to do what is shady, if not downright illegal, in order to amass a great fortune in this life.

But I wanted my kids to know, and God wants you to know that there is no disparity between prosperity and serving God. You can serve God and do everything legitimately, honestly, above board, and still achieve in this society. But you have to do it God's way.

So the servant knew it was God who made Abram rich, because Abram told him. Abram testified where and how he got his wealth. To me, the revelation of that Scripture was very important. So see, when I tell my congregation and other people that I minister to about how God has prospered me, it is sort of like I am speaking to my spiritual children. I don't tell about my blessings to be bragging. I want them to see what God has done for me and to know that He will do the same for them.

God wants all of His children to prosper, and likewise, I want my children — my biological and spiritual children — to prosper and be successful in all they do. So I share my testimony of God's goodness with them that same way.

Now this opens me up to criticism, but I do not mind the criticism. I can deal with that because I want to help as many people as I can so that they don't kill themselves because of their negative judgmental attitude towards my sharing these things. I want everyone to know that this is what the Lord has done and that you don't have to pull strings and do things under the table or sell your soul to the devil in order to succeed in life.

God has made everything in this world. The Lord created all the so-called wealth, but the devil learned how to control it. He has taken it out of the hands of the people of

God. Most of the people who have the wealth of this world are not Christians.

There is a way that you can attain prosperity, just like Abraham. Abraham was a tither. He paid tithes to Melchizedek. I want you to see that Abram was a man who shared his testimony about how great things the Lord had done for him.

Admittedly, people have attempted to use tithing as a gimmick. I once belonged to a church where the minister attempted to use tithing at one point in his ministry as a gimmick to get people to give more money to the church. The minister is dead now and I hope he went to be with the Lord. He had all kinds of gimmicks to bring in money. The choir, the usher board and all the other auxiliaries had to pay dues to raise money for the church coffers.

The pastor was always looking for another way to get folk to give money, and so he came up with this thing about tithing, where he used Malachi 3:8, which says, **Will a man rob God?** He wanted to put people under condemnation. He did not care anything about tithing and he did not explain anything about what tithing was all about.

I was a baby Christian and had just come into the things of God, and out of fear and also a desire to do what was right, I started tithing. I could not even pay my bills, yet I was attempting to tithe, even though the benefit of tithing was never explained. I certainly did not want to rob God, so I got scared.

But just because somebody has used tithing as a gimmick does not invalidate it. I do not care what some preacher may have done with it and how he may have misused it or abused It — that does not invalidate it as being God's way of blessing His people.

Genesis 28:14:

> **"...and in your seed all the families of the earth shall be blessed."**

Sounds like the same thing God said to Abraham, doesn't it? God did it through Abraham, through Isaac, through Jacob, and through the 12 sons or tribes, including Judah. And out of Judah came Christ and the whole world has been blessed because of Jesus.

Genesis 28:15-22:

> **"Behold, I am with you and will keep you wherever you go, and will bring you back to this land; for I will not leave you until I have done what I have spoken to you."**
>
> **Then Jacob awoke from his sleep and said, "Surely the LORD is in this place, and I did not know it."**
>
> **And he was afraid and said, "How awesome is this place! This is none other than the house of God, and this is the gate of heaven!"**
>
> **Then Jacob rose early in the morning, and took the stone that he had put at his head, set it up as a pillar, and poured oil on top of it.**
>
> **And he called the name of that place Bethel; but the name of that city had been Luz previously.**
>
> **Then Jacob made a vow, saying, "If God will be with me, and keep me in this way that I am going, and give me bread to eat and clothing to put on,**

107

"so that I come back to my father's house in peace, then the LORD shall be my God.

"And this stone which I have set as a pillar shall be God's house, and of all that You give me I will surely give a tenth to You."

Now why didn't he offer 15? Why didn't he say a 20th? A ninth? Why did he happen to come up with the same identical number that Abraham and Isaac used? Because his father taught him about tithing. He found out about it at home. He said, "I will surely give a tenth to you."

Tithing was still going on after Abraham, and the Law had not yet been given, because Moses hadn't come on the scene yet.

Tithing is the very foundation of God's financial plan, and if you learn how to get in line with that plan, you will be blessed and you will be a blessing.

You will be able to give and you will be able to receive. You will be able to give because you are a tither. I am a tither. I have been tithing now steadily without ever slacking off for well over 25 years.

Here is a small example, again, of how through tithing I have been blessed and, in turn, have been able to bless others:

Over a two-year period, I gave away four 40-inch television sets. They were my sets and they were like new, and I gave them away. Where did I get those television sets? The Lord gave them to me. He told me He would bless me and that I would be a blessing. So I gave those television sets away and the people who got them were blessed as a result of my being blessed.

How God's Financial Plan Works

How did I get things like that? I got them by tithing, because before I began tithing, my television set was repossessed. They came into the house, put the dolly under the thing, unplugged it, wrapped that cord around it and hauled that sucker out and put it on a truck! And I stood on the porch and said, "Bye, bye, TV."

The Lord has blessed me because of tithing, but I did not get into tithing to get. You have to guard your motives in everything you do relative to God. My desire is and always was to obey God. And I found out that in obeying, you get all the rest of the stuff. God said this very clearly in His Word, that if you be willing and obedient, you will eat the good of the land.

Some of you are willing, but you are not obedient. You are robbing God. You are willing to eat the good of the land, but he said two things: He said if you be willing *and* (not just willing *or* — if you want to eat the good of the land, it is not an option). He said if you be willing and obedient, you will eat the good of the land.

If God wants you to eat the good, He would want you to wear the good, to live in the good, to ride in the good, to have the good. He would not want you to eat the good and live in the bad.

Some people have been coming to church for years and have yet to put anything in the offering. And they are the main ones finding fault and criticizing when I talk about the things that God has done for me. They are yak-yak-yaking and running their ugly mouths, but not doing a thing to be willing and obedient. And they are getting their behinds kicked, and they are going to keep on getting kicked because they are not willing and obedient.

Some Christians would not give God 10 percent to save their scrawny, stingy, selfish necks.

They will go to a restaurant and give a perfect stranger a 15 percent tip. A person who has done nothing for them but their jobs. They are supposed to go to the kitchen and bring your food to the table. They are supposed to put water on the table. Yet, they get a 15 percent tip. But I wonder if Christians ever try calling them up in the midnight hour to see if that waiter or waitress will come over and cool the brow of a child who is feverish. Call the waiter to see if the waiter will come over and take care of your family disputes. See if the waiter or waitress will put up with your foolishness and your lackadaisical attitude. But the Lord will.

Their whole thinking is off. And that is why they are getting cheated out of life. That is why they are struggling. That is why they are working their buns off, sweating their brow and still not getting ahead. That is why they cannot seem to get it together. They have tried everything they know how, and it is still not working. I have news for them — it will never happen until they do it God's way.

If you are not a child of God and you are just a rank sinner, then Satan will work for you. But when you are a child of God, you are in an entirely different category, and there is more expected out of you. If you do not do what is right, God cannot help you, and the devil is out to gun you down. You have everything working against you.

Tithing is where it begins. It is the basis of God's financial plan. That is how the FaithDome was built — by faithful people. No gimmicks, no games, no chicken dinners, no rummage sales, no Thursday-night bingo games.

I do not know how God does it, but somehow He takes what might appear to be a little and He stretches it out to be a lot and does great things with it.

Despite that, you can ride around cities throughout the country and see preachers doing all kinds of gimmicks trying to raise money on Saturday afternoon, many using 50-gallon oil drums cut in half to barbecue chickens. What makes it so bad is they are out there selling stuff to sinners, as though God needs the support of sinners to keep His Church in business. It's a disgrace to God.

Don't misunderstand me — I do not say that to be judgmental or critical — but it is a travesty of divine justice to reduce our heavenly Father to the state of a beggar, as though the best God can do is barbecue on Saturday afternoon to raise enough money for His Church to stay open. But He will let us do it because He cannot do anything about it unless we do something about it.

But if you **be willing and obedient ...** it is an investment in the future and an investment for success!

I do not care where you are in life. If you are a child of God, if you start there — being willing and obedient — you can come out on top.

ELEVEN

CONSEQUENCES OF ROBBING GOD

I am a native Californian. I have never lived anywhere else but Los Angeles. I can remember when there was no such thing as homelessness. You did not see folk sleeping out on the streets, not like we see them today.

There is no need for anyone to be homeless. A lot of homelessness is a result of the curse that both the homeless and their parents have been living under. There is a curse. This whole nation is cursed, and that curse is very subtle. It is not like an atomic bomb. It does not occur as a big explosion. It can continue for generations in a family, and everybody in that family struggles.

I have known of persons who had good academic educations and they still could not make it financially. They became doctors or lawyers, yet they just did not achieve. They still were mediocre, never amounted to anything, still struggled, had family problems, divorces.

113

Nothing did them any good because they were operating in that curse.

You cannot rob God and get away with it. You might think you are getting away with it, but you are not. All you are doing is hurting yourself. God is going to be God when you go to bed and when you arise in the morning. He will be God when you live on the hill or in a penthouse and when you are sleeping under a freeway overpass.

You cannot cheat God. When you are gasping for your last breath, He will still be God. It is a fool's dream to think you can cheat the Almighty. So, you might as well get in on the program.

Procedures for Tithing

God has a financial plan, but there are rules, regulations, and procedures that govern this plan. And in order to participate and function in it on the highest level, we need to know how to do it. With God, we do not have to do things on a hit-and-miss, trial-and-error basis. You can learn some things by trial and error, but you can also get killed by trial and error, and that is not very profitable.

In Deuteronomy 8:18, as the children of Israel were preparing to go into the Promised Land, God said, once you get there, never forget that it is the Lord your God who gives you power to get wealth that He may establish His covenant.

I praise God that I found out about His financial plan and that by working His plan I am in a better position to serve Him, as well as be a channel of blessing in terms of ministry.

What is the tithing procedure? Let us find out now.

The children of Israel were given a mandate from the Father, as to how they were to bring their tithes and offerings before God.

You do not just walk into church and flip your offering envelope into the bucket. There is a way to bring the tithes and offerings to the Lord. There ought to be a proper attitude when we give, because it is a privilege and an honor to give to the heavenly Father.

God does not need anything we have. What can we do for God? God gives us the privilege to participate with Him in the Kingdom Age. That participation is not just to live right, not just to pray, not just to edify ourselves by praying in the Spirit, and not just to study the Bible. *Giving* is also a part of the Christian lifestyle, and there is a right and wrong way to do it. There is a way that produces results and a way that will not produce results.

Good Results of Tithing

I am a result-oriented person because I went for so many years without producing any good results. And once I found out that good results could be produced, I determined in my heart that every move I make is going to produce a positive result. This result would not only bring glory and honor to God, but would also push me up a little bit further in the things of God so that I could be a channel of blessing to other people. There is nothing better than being able to bless somebody or help someone.

HIGHER FINANCE

Deuteronomy 26:1:

"And it shall be, when you come into the land which the Lord your God is giving you as an inheritance, and you possess it and dwell in it."

That Scripture tells us that God gave them a land as an inheritance.

Notice the sequence: inherit, possess, dwell — not inherit and dwell. My point is that we are not the children of Israel. We are the Church of the Lord Jesus Christ. The natural question to arise is, "God gave the children of Israel a land, an inheritance. Do we have an inheritance, a place to possess, a place to dwell in? If so, where is it?"

Geographically speaking, Israel's physical land was Palestine. They were coming out of Egypt and they were going into Palestine. But what about us? Where is our land?

When I went to the Baptist church, they did not tell me about any land. They told me things such as, "I'm trying to get ready to put on my long white robe." They told me that after awhile, by and by, over there on the other side, we were going to walk through the pearly gates and talk to Peter, James and John about how we got over, and that we would "finally understand it better by and by." They told me that in the Baptist church, the Methodist church, the Presbyterian church, and the Christian and Missionary Alliance Church. Nobody told me anything about a land that God had already given me. So I was always looking to the future, always looking to getting it over there on the other side.

Now, over there on the other side is fine, but I am not over there on the other side. I am over here on this side, and

116

Consequences of Robbing God

I need to know whether I have a land so that I will know how to operate.

Do we have a land? Well, thank God we do.

Look at Colossians 1:12-13:

> **Giving thanks to the Father who has qualified us to be partakers of the inheritance of the saints in the light.**
> **He has delivered us from the power of darkness and conveyed us into the kingdom of the Son of His love.**

Now if God has qualified us to partake of the inheritance, then there must be an inheritance to partake of. Otherwise, there would not be a need to make us qualified to participate in something that does not exist.

There is similarity between the Israelites and the Christians: The Israelites were in bondage in Egypt against their will, and God brought them out of that captivity. God told Moses to go down and deliver them and bring them into a land that *I will show you*. Likewise, before we accepted Christ, we were in bondage to sin and darkness — *darkness* meaning the absence of the knowledge of God. That is where each one of us was in servitude before we became Christians. We were slaves.

Some of us still act as if we are slaves in some areas of our lives, even though we have been set free. We are still letting things that were out there in Egypt control our lives. We have been freed and given an inheritance, but we have to possess it and we have to dwell in it.

In Verse 13, the word *has* indicates that the time of the action has taken place. It is not taking place now, it is not

117

going to take place in the future. It *has* already taken place. That means we *are* delivered; we are not in bondage.

If we are not in bondage, we should not act as if we are in bondage and we should not accept anything that bondage has to offer us. The thing or things that used to control us should not control us anymore.

We should no longer be conditioned by whiskey, wine, beer, cigarettes, dope, drugs, pills, or sex. Those things were controlling our lives. That is bondage, and we have been delivered. That is why I do not have any patience with Christians who say, "Brother Price, I know it's wrong to smoke. I know that it's not Christian, but I've tried so hard to put those cigarettes down. I just can't seem to pass up those cigarette machines or the liquor store." Or, "I just drink a little every now and then."

But they are free! They do not have to try to get free. All they have to do is act as if they are free. Some people do not understand their covenant. They are busy trying to stop this or that. But they do not have to fight to stop anything; they simply don't have to do it any more. They are free.

If you have been in jail for 12 years and they parole you or pardon you, how much of a problem are you going to have not going back into that prison every week? In fact, you don't even want to see that prison. You don't want to know anything about what is going on in that prison. Would you have a temptation to go back in that prison and get back into your cell? No! Because you have been freed from it!

That wine bottle was a prison. That cigarette was a prison. Those pills were a prison. That dope was a prison. That cocaine was a prison. That sex was a prison. You have been pardoned. You have been freed. You have been let loose. Now either you are a liar and do not believe that, or you have never been really saved.

When I was younger, some guys and I fooled around and got into trouble. We stole a car and went what was called joy-riding. It's not much joy when you get caught. We were having us a high-heel time. We got caught and they put me in the local jail for 30 days. Now 30 days doesn't sound like a lot of time, but it is a lot of time when you are behind those bars.

I had flirted with crime. Nothing major like robbing a bank or killing somebody, but being in jail is being in jail and it is not nice! I did not like it. I used to look through the bars across the Los Angeles River and see people picnicking in the park. You know what I did? I made up my mind that when those 30 days were over, they would never get me in jail again.

Now that has been more than 46 years ago. From the day they let me out of jail after serving those 30 days until today, I have never been back on the street that jail is on. Never! When they opened that door, I did not know anything at that time about shaking the dust off my feet, but when I got out of that place, I shook everything off! I said, "You will never see me again in life!"

When the judge gave me the 30-day sentence in the courtroom, I started counting right then. They did not have to tell me when my day was to be released, I knew it was my day! It has been almost a lifetime ago and I have never been tempted to go back there.

Some Christians are lying to themselves. They don't really believe they are free and have been delivered. Have you ever been sick unto death, maybe with pneumonia or triple pneumonia, or some other illness that you were told you could die from? Have you ever had a temptation to go back and get sick again with it? I don't think so!

The only way the devil can tempt you with whatever you have been in bondage to is because you do not believe you have been delivered and are now free.

You still get that physical craving for the drug. You still get that feeling down in your private area which makes you think you have to go look up some former lover again. You will get those physical feelings and those emotions and the thoughts will come to your mind, but that is where by faith you have to say, "Oh, no, that is not for me. I am free!"

God has already legally provided your freedom from bondage. We read it in the 26th chapter of Deuteronomy.

The Israelites had to receive, possess and also dwell in the inheritance. So, by faith you have to dwell in your victory and in your freedom and in your deliverance. By faith you have to say, "Hey, I'm free. I cannot drink anymore, and I don't want to because it's against my better judgment and it's against the things of God." Alcohol cannot get out of the bottle and into you unless you put it into you.

Deuteronomy 26:13:

"Then you shall say before the LORD your God: 'I have removed the holy tithe from my house, and also have given them to the Levite, the stranger, the fatherless, and the widow, according to all Your commandments which You have commanded me; I have not transgressed Your commandments, nor have I forgotten them."

Every promise that God made to Israel was physical or material, not spiritual. He never promised them heaven and never said anything to them about heaven. God told them where their possession was — Palestine. On the other hand, He deals with the Body of Christ from a spiritual perspective that will ultimately end up in a physical manifestation.

The Kingdom of God is the land that we inherit. But, we have to possess it and we have to dwell in it. It is not enough just to have it.

We Are Not Left Destitute

I want to show you both in the Old and New Testaments that we have an inheritance. God has not left us destitute:

Deuteronomy 26:2-3:

> **"That you shall take some of the first of all the produce of the ground, which you shall bring from your land that the LORD your God is giving you, and put it in a basket and go to the place where the LORD your God chooses to make His name abide.**
>
> **"And you shall go to the one who is priest in those days, and say to him, 'I declare today to the LORD your God that I have come to the country which the LORD swore to our fathers to give us.'"**

Notice in Verse 2 He did not say to bring what is left over after you get through doing your thing. He is saying the Lord has given you this land — when you cultivate this land, plant it, and harvest it.

If you wonder where churches got the idea of using baskets, they got it from the Bible. God said, **... put it in a basket.**

And go to the place.... You take (1) *the firstfruit* (2) *put it in a basket* (3) *take it to the place.*

Where the Lord your God chooses. You do not choose it, God chooses it.

What does the word *place* mean? It indicates destination, location, area, worship center.

I was talking to this lady who thought that she was very cosmopolitan, very erudite and scholarly. She said she did not give to the church, but she said, "I do community service activities and I give to the hungry." And as she said this, she had her chest stuck out, so to speak. She wanted me to know she did give, but she gave to particular groups and to the needy.

All that is fine and you can do that with what belongs to you, but what we are talking about belongs to God. It is fine to give to organizations, but when you take the firstfruit, that belongs to God, and you had better put it where He chooses, not where *you* choose. Am I saying we should not give to the poor or to the homeless? I did not say that. We are talking about what belongs to God.

God gave them the land, they did not get the land on their own. That was God's gift, so He ought to have a right to say what to do with the firstfruit. And whoever does not like it should give back the land and go back into Egypt and slavery where they were before. How about that? Go back to your whiskey or wine bottle that was kicking your behind. Go back to that lust for sex that was running you crazy. Go back to your cigarettes that were stinking up you and your whole household, and causing you to breathe like a cow in distress! Go back to your pills that were dictating the terms of your lifestyle.

But if you want to stay in the land, then you are going to have to follow the orders of the man who owned the land and gave it to you.

You had better be sure of where you take your firstfruits and whether the Lord's name is there, or whether somebody is trying to pretend the Lord's name is there.

Notice that what was required of the children of Israel was ultimately also required of us under the New Covenant.

Deuteronomy 26:2:

"... **and go to the place where the** LORD **your God chooses to make His name abide.**"

What does that tell you? You are going to have to find the place where His name is. That is going to require some very serious investigation, and that is *your* responsibility.

It did not say that God is going to drag you there hollering and screaming with your gift in your hand. It did not say God is going to push you there. It says you have to go. It also tells you that if God's name was every place, you would not have to go and look. You could just close your eyes, and wherever you took that firstfruit, it would be God's place. But no, it said, ... **the place where the** LORD **your God chooses to make His name abide,** so that means He has not chosen to put His name everywhere.

In Deuteronomy 26:3, it says there is a priest we have to deal with.

"**And you shall go to the one who is priest in those days....**"

According to Hebrews 3:1, the high priest we have to deal with these days is Jesus:

Therefore, holy brethren, partakers of the heavenly calling, consider the Apostle and High Priest of our confession, Christ Jesus.

Let's read Deuteronomy 26:3 again.

"And you shall go to the one who is priest in those days, and say to him, 'I declare today to the LORD your God that I have come to the country which the LORD swore to our fathers to give us.' "

Can't you just put the tithe in a cup? He gave specific instructions — put it in a basket. Not an earthen jar, but a basket.

The tithe is the Lord's money and it does not belong to you. You can do whatever you want to do with *your* money — take it and flush it down the toilet if you want to — but you dare not do that with the Lord's money.

If His name is not there, then He did not choose it and you should not take your tithes there.

Is the Lord's Name There?

How in the world will we know where the Lord has chosen to place His name? A real simple way of evaluating that would be to find out whether God is being allowed to have first place. Where is His Word, His plan, His purpose, His will and His name being exalted above everything else? That is real easy to determine.

If God's name is there, there will be some evidence of God's life there. Very few churches actually have God's name there, even though they may be called a church.

We know He wants meat in His storehouse. Meat is whatever the people would need to grow spiritually. How does meat get in God's house? By tithing. Any church that does not promote and focus on tithes as the way to bring meat into God's house, God did not put His name there. So that narrows it down to just a few.

Notice it does not say in Malachi, "Bring me all the chickens into My house," or "Bring all the bingo cards into My house," or "Bring all the Katydid candy into My house." You have to ask yourself: "Does that church honor God's Word and God's request in terms of how to have meat in His house?" Very few churches do. They usually tell you what *they* believe. They won't tell you what the Bible says. They say, "This is what we believe. This is the way we teach it."

All of those are little signposts along the way that ought to alert you to whether or not God's name is there. Simply because the thing is called the house of God does not make it the house of God. You have to check it out. It can look good, have great music, great choirs, great soloists, a lot of rocking and rolling, but it does not mean God is there.

You have to look at where God's Word finds its place in that ministry. What is first, God's Word, or "the way we have always done it?" Does the Bible dictate the terms of their actions?

Many places will tell you they do not believe in speaking with tongues. The Lord's name is not in that church. God believes in speaking in tongues. You don't, but you say God's name is there.

"We don't believe in speaking with tongues in our church." I know you don't in *your* church. But we are trying to find out about *God's* church. If His name is there, then everything that supports His name ought to be there too.

I have heard preachers say, "We don't believe in tithing, or in speaking with tongues." They don't believe the gifts of the spirit are for us today. Well, friend, God's name is apparently not there.

There are many other things you could look at to determine if His name is there.

Hebrews 6:17-20:

> **Thus God, determining to show more abundantly to the heirs of promise the immutability of His counsel, confirmed it by an oath,**
>
> **that by two immutable things, in which it is impossible for God to lie, we might have strong consolation, who have fled for refuge to lay hold of the hope set before us.**
>
> **This hope we have as an anchor of the soul, both sure and steadfast, and which enters the Presence behind the veil,**
>
> **where the forerunner has entered for us, even Jesus, having become High Priest forever according to the order of Melchizedek.**

There is not much in the Bible about Melchizedek. But what we know is that he was apparently a priest. And when Abram came back from rescuing his nephew Lot, who had been taken captive, Melchizedek suddenly appeared on the scene and Abram gave him tithes. The reason that Jesus is typed after Melchizedek is because as far as genealogy was

concerned, nobody knew where Melchizedek came from.
Nobody had any record of his beginning, or about his end-
ing. It was as if he just suddenly appeared and later — 'zip!'
— disappeared. So they say Melchizedek did not have a
beginning and he did not have an end. We know he did, but
there was no record found of it.

And like Melchizedek, Jesus has an unending priesthood. Since Melchizedek did not die, he continued to be
priest. At least this is the way people thought of it, simply
because they could not find any evidence of his appearing
or where he went. So, Jesus is like that, in that He has an
unending priesthood.

Hebrews 7:1-9:

> **For this Melchizedek, king of Salem, priest of
> the Most High God, who met Abraham returning
> from the slaughter of the kings and blessed him,**
>
> **to whom also Abraham gave a tenth part of
> all, first being translated "king of righteousness,"
> and then also king of Salem, meaning "king of
> peace,"**
>
> **without father, without mother, without gene-
> alogy, having neither beginning of days nor end of
> life, but made like the Son of God, remains a priest
> continually.**
>
> **Now consider how great this man was, to whom
> even the patriarch Abraham gave a tenth of the
> spoils.**
>
> **And indeed those who are of the sons of Levi,
> who receive the priesthood, have a commandment**

to receive tithes from the people according to the law, that is, from their brethren, though they have come from the loins of Abraham;

but he whose genealogy is not derived from them received tithes from Abraham and blessed him who had the promises.

Now beyond all contradiction the lesser is blessed by the better.

Here mortal men receive tithes, but there he receives them, of whom it is witnessed that he lives.

Even Levi, who receives tithes, paid tithes through Abraham, so to speak.

The word *tithes* is mentioned eight times in this chapter. The Bible says in the mouth of two or three witnesses let every word be established. Here, you have eight references to tithes. That ought to tell you something.

When we bring our tithes and our offerings, we present them to Jesus our high priest, and under this New Covenant and in this spiritual kingdom He takes those gifts before our Father. He ministers on behalf of the people. Not on behalf of Himself.

The people of Israel were supposed to say something to the priest, not just go in mute. This means that time is involved. We should not just run in the church door and throw the offering in a basket behind the door or by the door. Some churches have done this. In fact, I know of some churches that stopped receiving offerings. They just put a basket at the back and tell people, "If you want to give, just give something on the way out." But that is not the way the Bible tells us to do it.

Consequences of Robbing God

It was necessary to present the tithes and offerings in a particular manner because there was abuse and misuse of the manner in which tithes and offerings were received.

Instead of the churches doing it the way God said do it, they made a spectacle out of it. They would bring a little table in front, and the deacons would stand behind the table and have everybody marching around. Some churches still do that today, and all of it is a gimmick. It is designed to bring about guilt. Nobody wants to physically get up in the presence of everybody in the congregation and *not* put something in the basket. You just feel bad about doing it.

But ministers have the mentality that if you con the people and get them up there publicly, nobody would dare not put something on the table. That was all designed to get people to give more money, but you do not have to do that when you do it God's way.

At some of those churches where they have that table up front and they don't get all the money they need, they will say such things as, "We got $25.89. We need eleven cents. Can we get eleven cents?" Then someone gives a quarter, and now they are over the $26, and now they need another 86 cents to make it even. That kind of thing would go on and on and on. It was a farce, a disgrace before God. That is not His way.

From the inception of my ministry, our church never had that kind of setup, yet all of our needs were and are still met by doing it God's way. No gimmicks, no games, just tell the people to tithe.

Nobody checks to find out if you are tithing, unless you are applying to work in one of our helps ministry organizations, or in a leadership position. In that case, you should be leading by doing what the Word says. If you do not want to be checked on, you should not want to be in a leadership position. Other than that, nobody is walking around behind you to find out if you are a tither. If you do not tithe, that is between you and the Lord.

But people will never be able to say that they attended Crenshaw Christian Center and never heard about tithing, because tithing is God's way, that is the way He wants things done. We get the benefit of the tithe, because the church operates through the tithes.

The children of Israel were supposed to profess something, say something. Beginning with Verse 5 of Deuteronomy 26, you will see what they professed.

Deuteronomy 26:5-11:

> **"And you shall answer and say before the LORD your God: 'My father was a Syrian, about to perish, and he went down to Egypt and dwelt there, few in number; and there he became a nation, great, mighty, and populous.**
>
> **'But the Egyptians mistreated us, afflicted us, and laid hard bondage on us.**
>
> **'Then we cried out to the LORD God of our fathers, and the LORD heard our voice and looked on our affliction and our labor and our oppression.**
>
> **'So the LORD brought us out of Egypt with a mighty hand and with an outstretched arm, with great terror and with signs and wonders.**
>
> **'He has brought us to this place and has given us this land, "a land flowing with milk and honey";**

'and now, behold, I have brought the firstfruits
of the land which you, O Lᴏʀᴅ, have given me.'
Then you shall set it before the Lᴏʀᴅ your God,
and worship before the Lᴏʀᴅ your God.

"So you shall rejoice in every good thing which the
Lᴏʀᴅ your God has given to you and your house, you
and the Levite and the stranger who is among you."

What they were to profess or confess was basically a
cataloging of where they had come from — how God called
Abraham and how Abraham obeyed God, and about Isaac
and Jacob and the 12 tribes of Israel. Because we forget and
become so comfortable and so satisfied, it dulls the edge of
our appreciation for where we are.

So in bringing the tithe every week, it reminds us of
where we have come from, of what we have now. I like to
do that. My wife and I often sit and talk about where we are
now and we look around and see how the Lord has blessed
us, how He has honored His Word. We think about what
we used to have, what we did not have, and what we could
not do and what we can do now. We think about what we
are involved in now and what we were involved in then,
and it does something to you.

By doing that, you can never become complacent about
where you are. You should always be consciously aware of
where you came from — not dwelling on the past, not going back to the "good old days," because they were often
not so good.

But when you remember where you came from, your
heart fills with gratitude. Mine does. Every time I walk into
a store to buy something, it feels good to realize I do not

have to put something on a charge card and make monthly payments. It might not be a big thing for you, but is a big thing for me.

So the Bible says when the children of Israel went to the high priest they were to say something. And we, under the New Covenant, are supposed to say something too.

This is the profession our Crenshaw Christian Center congregation makes when bringing their tithes:

"Heavenly Father, we profess this day to You, that we have come into the inheritance which You swore to give us. We are in the land which You have provided for us in Jesus Christ, the Kingdom of Almighty God. We were sinners serving Satan, he was our god. But we called upon the Name of Jesus, and You heard our cry and delivered us from the power of darkness and translated us into the Kingdom of Your dear Son.

"Jesus, as our Lord and High Priest, we bring the firstfruits of our income to You, that you may worship the Lord our God with them. Father, we rejoice in all the good which You have given to us and to our households. We have heard Your voice and have done according to all that You have commanded us.

"Now, Father, as you look down from Your holy habitation from heaven, to bless us as You said in Your Word, we believe that we now receive those blessings according to Your Word. This is our confession of faith. In Jesus' name."

TWELVE

THE LAW OF SOWING AND REAPING

Malachi 3, which we have read, gives us the background for God's financial plan. You see, there is no receiving without giving. That is just a divine law, and it works in every area of life, whether you are a Christian or not.

The Bible calls it the law of sowing and reaping. No matter what you sow, you will reap a result — and the reaping is always multiplied from what you sowed. You cannot sow one corn seed and get a stalk with only one grain of corn on it. You get several ears with many grains. There is multiplication in sowing and reaping.

So if you want to receive from God, you have to sow into the things of God.

It is important that a person not become mercenary about this. We want our motive to be that we love our Father because we appreciate what He has done for us. He took us when nobody else wanted us. When the world was kicking our backsides and telling us we were unworthy and that we did not measure up, the Father God took us in as we were.

He did not tell us to clean up first and then come. He took us dirty, failing, messed up, scared, defeated, whipped. He took us in and He loved us, not because of us, but in spite of us. So, out of gratitude, out of love, and out of a desire to be obedient, we should want to give — not to get, but out of love and obedience.

Now once our purpose and reason for giving is settled, then we would be foolish if we did not take advantage of what God has built into the system to be a channel to bless us so that we could become a blessing.

He made the statements in Malachi for the Israelites, but it applies to all generations:

Malachi 3:10-11:

> **"Bring all the tithes into the storehouse,**
> **That there may be food in My house,**
> **And try Me now in this,"**
> **Says the LORD of hosts,**
> **"If I will not open for you the windows of heaven**
> **And pour out for you such blessing**
> **That there will not be room enough to receive it.**
> **"And I will rebuke the devourer for your sakes,**
> **So that he will not destroy the fruit of your ground,**

**Nor shall the vine fail to bear fruit for you
in the field,"
Says the LORD of hosts."**

Here is God Almighty giving us a challenge. Challenging us in the one place where we have the greatest degree of problems, and that is with our finances. Most people do not want to turn their money loose quickly. And most people do not have enough of it. They want more. They are trying to get more.

God made a covenant that says He is going to bless us so that we can become a blessing. Realistically, you cannot afford to give away what you do not have. So if your own needs are going unmet, it is somewhat fallacious to meet someone else's needs.

Sometimes Christians get this euphoric idea of thinking things are going to fall out of heaven, but money comes through the hands of men.

Because of Adam's rebellion and failure to follow the things of God, it caused the control and the dominion of things like money, gold and silver to fall into the hands of the person we call Satan. So what God has been attempting to do through the years is regain control of that wealth so that His covenant can be established. But Satan has very cleverly infiltrated denominations, theology, and tradition, and has sold the Church of the Lord Jesus Christ a bill of goods.

He has tricked the Church into believing that there is something intrinsically godly about deprivation and poverty. He tells them that they will get theirs on the other side, so they really should not be concerned about getting any more in this life than just enough to barely make it. And while he is saying that, he (Satan) and his cohorts are controlling the world and using up the resources that the Father put here for His people. Instead of the children of God getting the benefit out of it, Satan gets the benefit out of it.

So that is the backdrop for all that we are talking about in terms of God's financial plan.

Operating in God's Principles

You have no idea until you get there about the joy in being able to afford the things that you need and desire.

I do not care if you are making $100,000 a year. If you are not careful, you will end up living up to your $100,000 and still be just as whipped and strapped as somebody who only makes $10,000 a year.

If you do not learn to operate in the principles of God's Word, Satan will keep you on a treadmill, just like a guinea pig on a treadmill, never getting where you want to go.

So we need to learn how to become financially independent of the circumstances.

The economic systems are controlled by satanic influence. That is why the distribution of the wealth is so unequal. You can see that God has nothing to do with it, because if He did, then all the millionaires would be Christians — not sinners. Then God could speak to their hearts to have them do deeds that would help humanity.

The Body of Christ has to come to a place where we can gain back the wealth so that we can distribute it and allow God to establish His covenant.

Tithing is the trigger of the gun, so to speak, that releases the projectile of prosperity.

If you can believe that the 23rd Psalm, which is found in the Old Testament, is for us today, then why can't you believe that tithing is for New Covenant people? In other words, if you are going to accept one facet of truth from the Old Covenant, then you must be fair and willing at least to accept other facets of truth.

God made that statement in Malachi 3 to the children of Israel. However, its truth is for all generations of Believers, up until the time that Jesus returns to visibly and physically set up His earthly Kingdom.

Look at Mark 16:17:

"In My name they will cast out demons...."

There is only one devil, but there are many demons. Notice in that verse it does not say anything about what God is going to do with those demons. It says, ... **these signs will follow them that believe: In My name they will cast out demons....** Who shall? The Believer. Not God, not Jesus, not the Holy Spirit. Believers.

Ephesians 4:27:

Nor give place to the devil.

Who is supposed to not give place? Christians. In other words, He is telling us that the devil cannot have a place unless we give it to him.

James 4:7:

Therefore submit to God. Resist the devil and he will flee from you.

Notice in all three cases, it is up to the Believer to do something about the devil or demons. However, in Malachi God is saying that He will take care of the devil. But He cannot and He will not take care of the devil unless you get involved relative to your finances.

If you bring the tithe into the storehouse, He said, "*I will…*" He did not tell you to resist the devil at that point. He does not tell you to "give him no place" at that point. And He does not tell you to cast him out. He says if you will bring the tithe into the storehouse, **"I will rebuke the devourer for your sakes..."**

When you have God on your side, you have somebody on your side! Can you understand that? But it is only in reference to tithing.

What did it say about the ground? **He will not destroy the fruit of your ground.** Remember, Israel was an agrarian society, sheepherders. They lived off the land. We do not live off the land — at least most of us do not. Our ground is not the field, or the cattle. Our ground is the computer, the service station, the bakery, the meat market, the car lot. Our ground is wherever we lawfully earn our living. We plant our labor, we plant our time, we plant our energy and we get a harvest in return — our paycheck every week or every month. That's our harvest.

I can look back over my own life and see the times when I made money and that money quickly disappeared. It seemed as if it was never enough, no matter how much I got. It seemed that something would happen every minute to take that money. If I got a little extra, something would break down. That is how Satan can get into your circumstances and steal the fruit of your ground — the money you have earned.

I want you to see something here: If God Almighty is the One who will rebuke the devourer, then God Almighty must not be the devourer. God is not your problem, but He has been blamed for it.

In Malachi 3:11, it says: **"I will rebuke the devourer...."** So there must be a devourer.

... rebuke the devourer ... and he will not....

Notice the Scripture does not say *it* shall not, but rather, **"he will not..."** That's a personal pronoun. That is talking about a person. It is talking about Satan. He is the one who will destroy your fruit. He is the one who would steal from you. Jesus said Satan was a thief, a robber, and a murderer from the very beginning.

He will steal your finances. You can work your fingers to the bone and never have enough if you are not a tither. You should not decide to tithe simply because God will rebuke the devourer for you. You should tithe because (1) it is right to do it, (2) you say you love Him and you want to be obedient, and (3) this is God's financial plan. You want to operate in the context of His plan and tithing is part of that plan. Tithing is at the crux of it. In tithing, Satan's power is broken over you financially. Remember, the tithe belongs to God.

Malachi 3:8:

> **"Will a man rob God?**
> **Yet you have robbed Me!**
> **But you say,**

139

'In what way have we robbed You?'
In tithes and offerings."

If you are not tithing, you are a God-robber and should be arrested and put in jail. Isn't that what we do with people who rob banks?

Disobedience and Unwillingness

Look at Verse 9 and you will understand the possible reason for any financial dilemma you may be having:

"You are cursed with a curse,
For you have robbed Me,
Even this whole nation."

I lived that out in my own life for years and I did not understand what was happening. I thought it was the system, I thought it was the white folk. No point in lying about it, that is what I thought. They had all the money and I did not have any. I figured they were the ones doing it to me. I found out they were not the ones, they were not the problem. It is not the black ones or the white ones or the red, brown or green ones! It is Satan who is the problem, but he has no place in you unless you give it to him. And the way you give it to him is by your disobedience and unwillingness to do it God's way.

Disobedience opens the door and allows Satan to back his truck up into your life and haul off everything that belongs to you.

I do not care how much I worked. If I worked overtime, the overtime got eaten up and did not do that much good. I still didn't have enough. You know why? I was robbing God, and as a result I was operating under the curse and didn't even know it.

Ignorance of the law is no excuse — even if you do not know something. It will still work against you. You can walk through a dark room and not realize it has no flooring, not knowing it has a 300-foot hole, yet you are still going down. So ignorance of the law is no excuse.

The Tithe Is an Obligation

You *give* an offering, but you *pay* the tithe. The tithe belongs to God. It is His. It is an obligation, and it is one you ought to want to do. You should love to do it when you find out the benefits of it.

Tipping at a restaurant used to be 10 percent; it went up to 15 percent, and more than that in some places. God has never raised His percentage! It has been 10 percent for 6,000 years. And look at the benefits you get for tipping God:

Psalm 91:16 says:

**"With long life will I satisfy him,
And show him My salvation."**

You get divine healing, salvation, the Word of God, heaven, the Holy Spirit, angels around you, protection everywhere you go. Why wouldn't you want to give God a tip?

Think about it: The richest being in the universe adopted you.

Just con yourself and think of it as tipping instead of tithing. Once you get into it, you will love it. You cannot beat God giving.

HIGHER FINANCE

Proverbs 3:9-10:

> **Honor the LORD with your possessions,**
> **And with the firstfruits of all your increase;**
> **So your barns will be filled with plenty,**
> **And your vats will overflow with new wine.**

Do you think God Almighty is worthy of honor from us? We get a paycheck — that is our fruit. These verses go right along with tithing. Tithing should come off the top. Notice that it does not say, honor the Lord with your fruit, but it specifies firstfruit. We have the habit of giving God what is left over — sort of like we do the dog. We give Fido and Rover the scraps. People put a dollar in the offering plate and think they have done God a favor.

It would be something if God asked for 90 percent and left you with just 10 percent. That might be a little difficult to deal with, but all God asks for is one dime out of a dollar. As a result of tithing, He said, He will rebuke the devourer for your sake, and he will not destroy your fruit in the ground before its time. No bank will give you that kind of service.

In Malachi 3:10, God says:

> **"And try Me now in this,"**
> **Says the LORD of hosts,**
> **"If I will not open for you the windows of heaven**
> **And pour out for you such blessing**
> **That there will not be room enough to receive it."**

142

The Law of Sowing and Reaping

Two Things Tithing Provides

Two things are provided by the tithe. First the Gospel is supported, and secondly, you are blessed.

If you have made a commitment to God, then you have committed to do His will. And if you have committed to do His will, a part of His will is to **bring all the tithes into the storehouse....**

Proverbs 3:9-10 is talking about honoring Him with your substance. Substance is tangibility — materiality. Substance is that which can be perceived by your senses. It is something you can see, smell, hear, taste, or touch.

If you are still hung up on some denominational or traditional or theological concept and cannot bring yourself to tithe because you are convinced that it is Old Covenant, then do it out of honor. Has honor gone out? Is honor Old Testament? I hear the writer of the New Covenant saying give honor to whom honor is due. How much honor is the heavenly Father due?

The field cannot bless you with a crop of corn until you first put some seed into the ground. Likewise, you must plant with your tithe if you want the harvest.

That is the law of sowing and reaping. You do not get anything until you make an investment. You don't get a paycheck until you invest 40 hours, generally speaking. When you go to a grocery store, you get no groceries until you put money on the counter. You have to give before you can receive. That goes for every area of life. We give and receive. What is the big deal?

Out of that receiving, we then get more to give, more seed in other words to plant, to sow, and it has a cumulative

143

effect. It goes on and on and on, gets bigger and bigger and bigger.

The first reason for giving is to support the ministry. We have no products, per se, to sell — no heavenly deodorant, no Holy Ghost detergent, no angelic cologne. We have to depend simply on freewill giving.

When we give according to God's plan and purpose, it will not come off as begging, gimmicks or games. It will be done in a very precious, but a very honorable way, and tithing is the way. It should be taught throughout the church world.

If we tithe — give according to the Word of God — we produce results that are far exceeding those of barbecues, rummage sales, and bingo games.

Where Should You Pay the Tithe?

Some people are really confused about where to pay the tithe. Some preachers will say that the tithe automatically goes to the local church.

I received a letter on this subject from a person who views my *Ever Increasing Faith* television program. She was questioning whether I should be suggesting that viewers send me tithes and offerings. She felt if they did that, I would be taking away from the local church. But I also know that there are multitudes of Christians who watch my television program who do not have a church home. They do not go to church because they have not found a church in their area that is meeting their spiritual need.

In Hebrews 10:25, the Lord says:

**Not forsaking the assembling of ourselves to-
gether, as is the manner of some...**

But you have to be choosy about where you go to
church. I do not know about you, but I do not go to church
just to be going to church. You need to go to a church where
you are not just being entertained by good music, because
when the economic wolf comes knocking on your door to
foreclose on your house, you cannot go play the *Hallelujah
Chorus* and get the circumstances changed.

Music is great and I love it, but if good music is all that
you get out of going to church, then you have wasted your
time, because you can buy a tape and listen to good music.
You ought to go to church to be fed spiritually. God's Word
is spiritual food.

Jesus said in John 6:63, "**... The words that I speak to
you are spirit, and they are life.**" That simply means that
God's Words are addressed to man's spirit, not to man's intellect. And those words, if you will listen and act on them,
are like eating food. They will nourish you spiritually just
like eating will nourish you physically.

So, where should we pay the tithe? Should it be to the
local church? Well, yes and no. It all depends. A local
church, to qualify for receiving the tithe must be God's
house, where the meat of God's Word is on deposit so that
those who go there on a weekly basis can be fed out of the
treasure of that Word.

The church I went to after I was converted was a place
where the pastor was always looking for gimmicks to get
the people to give money. We were never taught how to
give based on the Word of God. And there was nothing

145

ever taught about faith, about giving and believing you receive. I never heard that. He just used one statement, a tithing gimmick, **Will a man rob God?** to put us in bondage and we gave out of guilt. But honey, that church did not qualify for the tithe. There was no meat of God's Word there. All kinds of underhanded, ungodly things were going on. People in positions of authority were involved in illicit affairs. The church simply did not qualify for the tithe.

The local church should qualify so that when the children of God come, they can receive something that they can take with them and apply to their daily life situations. That church I went to did not qualify for the tithe. I could not even pay my bills, yet I began tithing out of guilt and fear that God was going to drop the hammer on me if I did not tithe. The local church does not have a right to the tithe *unless* it conforms to God's plan and purpose.

A tithe is not an offering. A tithe is a debt that one owes to God. That tithe belongs to God. Therefore, that makes you a trustee. A trustee functions as the guardian. You are a trustee over the tithe. God is going to hold you and me accountable for our stewardship of the tithe. You are going to have to give an account to God for what you do with His possessions. So you ought to be very prudent about what you do with that tithe. You should know where and what you are putting that tithe into.

Deuteronomy 26:12-14

"When you have finished laying aside all the tithe of your increase in the third year — the year of tithing — and have given it to the Levite, the

stranger, the fatherless, and the widow, so that they may eat within your gates and be filled,

"then you shall say before the L ORD your God: 'I have removed the holy tithe from my house, and also have given them to the Levite, the stranger, the fatherless, and the widow, according to all Your commandments which You have commanded me; I have not transgressed Your commandments, nor have I forgotten *them.*

'I have not eaten any of it when in mourning, nor have I removed *any* of it for an unclean use, nor given *any* of it for the dead. I have obeyed the voice of the L ORD my God, and have done according to all that You have commanded me.' "

This was specifically for Israel — not something He asks the Church to do.

You and I are trustees who are going to have to examine where we put the tithe. Ask yourself the question, "If I go and present myself to this church to be ministered to, what am I being given from God's Word?"

147

THIRTEEN

Do Not Pay
Tithe to the Dead

When I think back to the church that I started out in, I recall that the minister was an excellent speaker who began as a boy preacher. And over the years he had learned to whoop and holler. He was good, but when I go back and examine the content of what I was getting, it was death. It was not life. Something can sound good and have no life in it. So ask yourself when you go to a church, what do you receive? Are you getting the meat of God's word? Is God's meat in this house? If not, then it is a dead church and you have no business giving the tithe to the dead.

Any church that denies the Holy Spirit in the sanctuary or in the members who come to that sanctuary, that is a dead church. Because Zechariah 4:6 says " 'Not by might nor by power, but by My Spirit,' says the Lord of hosts." Now if the Holy Spirit is not permitted to have His way, then what happens in that church is not going to be by His Spirit. It will be by whatever the people come up with.

Where a church denies the Holy Spirit to have free course, and when a minister denies people the right to be filled with the Spirit according to the New Testament, but would rather take his own denominational, theological view and tradition over what the Bible says, that is a dead church. And if you put your tithes into that church, you are a fool and you are going to answer to God for what you do with what belongs to Him. This is God's money.

If you place your tithe in a church that does not believe in divine healing, you will have to give an account to God. The people in such a church might not even be saved. I say that because a part of what Jesus suffered on that cross was for sickness and disease. That is the same Jesus Christ they say they love, and One they say they follow and say is their Savior and Lord and Redeemer and High Priest. Any church that does not pray for the sick is dead. You have no right to put the tithe in that church.

If you look at the life of Jesus, you will find that He spent most of His time healing people — casting out demons, cleansing the lepers, opening the eyes of the blind. It is obvious that God does not want our bodies malfunctioning. The Bible says that our bodies are the temples of the Holy Spirit. The Bible says that Jesus Christ is the head and we are the Body of Christ.

It is interesting to note that Jesus walked the earth for three-and-one-half years in His public ministry and never allowed sickness or disease to dominate His body. At that time He had not yet paid the redemption price. Man was not yet redeemed. He had not died. He had not risen from the dead. He had not ascended to the Father, and the New Covenant had not come in. Think about it, Jesus actually ministered under the Old Covenant. The Old Covenant was still in operation until such time as Jesus said from the cross, "It is finished." That did not mean salvation was finished because He had not died yet, but what was finished was the Law, the Old Covenant.

Since Jesus would not allow sickness and disease in His body then, why would He allow sickness and disease in His Body today, now that He has defeated the enemy, now that He has paid the redemption price and now that He is seated at the right hand of the Father as our High Priest? Why would He want sickness and disease in His Body now?

Matthew 8:17 says:

"... he Himself took our infirmities and bore our sicknesses."

And 1 Peter 2:24 says:

who Himself bore our sins in His own body on the tree, that we, having died to sins, might live for righteousness — by whose stripes you were healed.

Let me give you a little theological exposé, because there have been some preachers who have cheated their people out of the benefits of divine healing by saying that 1 Peter 2:24 does not refer to physical healing, but rather spiritual healing.

I challenge anybody anywhere, anytime to show me Scripture in the Bible from Genesis to Revelation where it ever refers to God healing people spiritually. They cannot. It does not mention "spiritual healing" in there.

151

First Peter 2:24 could not be talking about spiritual healing because man's problem relative to God is not spiritual sickness, it is spiritual death (if you go back to what God said to Adam and Eve in the garden of Eden). Man is not sick spiritually; man is dead spiritually. He is cut off from God, alienated from God. He does not need healing, he needs life.

Jesus said He came not to take any man's life, but to give him life. He never said anything about coming to make somebody well spiritually.

Spirits cannot be healed. A spiritually dead man does not need healing, he needs life. Jesus said I came that they might have life — not healing for the spirit — but life.

When Adam sinned, he did not get sick. God never said, in the day you eat you shall surely get sick. He said, when you eat, you are going to die. And when Adam ate, he died spiritually and began to die physically. Spiritual death is instantaneous. Physical death is progressive.

Man needs regeneration; man needs to be made new.

Second Corinthians 5:17 does not say if any man be in Christ, he is a healed spirit. It says, if any man be in Christ, he is a brand-new creature.

Any church that does not teach divine healing is dead. And you do not have any business putting God's money into that dead thing to continue to perpetuate it. It ought to die and get out of the way so that those who are alive can get on with the program.

I am not calling names of any denominations. You are the ones who have to make the decisions, but you have to have adequate, accurate information on which to base your decision. He said, do not give any of that tithe to the dead. And it is a dead church that doesn't teach you about divine healing — which is part of your covenant rights, part of your redemptive package, which is what Jesus died for.

Jesus took upon Himself the sicknesses, not only the sickness and disease of the physical body, but your sins. God wants you well and He wants you saved. If a church doesn't teach that, it is dead and you are a fool for going there, let alone putting God's money — the tithe — there.

I know someone will not like what I have said, but the truth will make you free. Lying and cheating are not going to make us free. We need the truth. Jesus said if you continued in His Word, you are His disciples, indeed, and you will know the truth and the truth would make you free. That's the Bible. He did not say if you continue in the denomination or in theology or in tradition.

God Never Changes

One of our Father's names is Jehovah Rapha, which means, "I am the Lord who heals you." The Bible says that God never changes, so whatever He was yesterday, He is today. And whatever He is today, He will be tomorrow and forever — because He is the same yesterday, today, and forever. If He is the Lord that healed yesterday, He would have to be the Lord that heals today, tomorrow and forever. If that is not true then He changed and we would have to rewrite the Bible.

Some people come to church with sick bodies and leave with sick bodies because the church gives them no hope. All it does is say, "Hold on, hang in there. After a while by and by it will be better." That is not the Gospel!

153

If you go back through Matthew, Mark, Luke, and John and examine every situation where anybody came to Jesus with a need for physical healing, you will not find one place where He turned them away.

I started out in the Baptist Church — and this is not a putdown of Baptists — but we never prayed for the sick in our church. And I know other people who were and still are in the Baptist church and they do not pray for the sick in their church either. If they do, it is a rare church.

So that kind of church has no right to the tithe — and if you give it, you are giving God's tithe to the dead and you are going to pay for it. You are going to answer to God for it.

If I am not telling the truth, all you have to do is point the Scripture out and say, "Pastor Price, you are wrong." I have no problem changing, and I change instantaneously. I want to be right. I do not want to be thought right and find out later that I am wrong. I have never said that I am perfect. However, I want to be and I'm working on it. Somebody has to be right, and it might as well be me. I give you that same privilege to be right. The bottom line is the Word is right, so whoever lines up with the Word, that person is right, be they male or female.

Some people are not going to like the next statement I make either, but I might as well just rock the whole boat. Any church that does not believe in being filled with the Holy Spirit and speaking with other tongues is a church full of people that are unsaved. They have to be spiritually dead. They could not be spiritually alive, because if they were alive with the same Holy Spirit, they would have to believe in the power of the Holy Spirit. How can you be born of the Holy Spirit and not believe in the power of the Holy Spirit?

154

It has to qualify as a storehouse before the tithe can be given to that local congregation. It should not get the tithe just because it is a local church.

Deuteronomy 26:14:

> **I have not eaten any of it when in mourning, nor have I removed any of it for an unclean *use*, nor given *any* of it for the dead. I have obeyed the voice of the LORD my God, and have done according to all that You have commanded me.**

In the Amplified Bible it says, **I have not eaten of the tithe in my mourning [making the tithe unclean], nor have I handled any of it when I was unclean, nor given any of it to the dead.**

I like that because it specifically points out what the principle is that is being dealt with. He said I have not given any of it to the dead.

Jesus is about life.

The New Covenant clearly reveals your covenant privileges and your covenant rights. In other words, the things that belong to you, the things that God wants you to have and enjoy are in the New Covenant.

If you went and looked at what they call their statement of faith, you would find out that there are a lot of things that most churches do not teach; they claim to believe it but they do not promote these things. They do not teach them to their people, so the people can never take advantage of them. You cannot take advantage of what you do not know.

We do not have time to gamble with our lives. If a church is anointed by the Holy Spirit, and called by God to be a channel through which His Word goes forth to His people, then that Word ought to cover all that God placed in His covenant for the benefit of His people.

Mark 16:17:

"And these signs will follow those who believe: In My name they will cast out demons; they will speak with new tongues."

If you are not a Believer, the signs won't follow. But if you are a Believer, the signs will follow you. Either that is true or Jesus lied to us. And the Bible in John 14 says that He is **"the way, the truth, and the life."** So if the signs don't follow, then those who say they believe are lying. They do not believe because the signs do not follow.

Now that does not mean that persons that used to curse and swear can't change and start talking nice. The word *tongues* in Mark 16 is a Greek word called *glossa,* and it means "language." That has direct reference to the infilling of the Holy Spirit.

What we're doing is qualifying who is dead and who is alive. If a church is alive, then it will proclaim the full counsel of the covenant of God.

I do not care if you have been a member of a church for 25 years. You have been going to the wrong church for 25 years if they do not teach the full counsel of the covenant of God.

We are not dealing with the sincerity or the lack of sincerity of individual people. There are plenty of good people, lovely people who are born again and love the Lord, but they just do not know the Word. That is all. They are as sincere as they can be, but they do not know the Word.

Do Not Pay Tithe to the Dead

I did not always know the Word, and most Christians did not always know the Word. I was as ignorant as I could be of the Word when I was in the Baptist, Methodist and Presbyterian churches. They never taught me the Word. I was saved and that is about it. I do not mean to diminish the importance of salvation, but you have to understand that salvation encompasses more than just being born again. It also encompasses a total life lived in victory to the glory and honor of God. It is all a part of the same package.

Let's read Acts 1:4:

And being assembled together with them, He commanded them not to depart from Jerusalem, but to wait for the Promise of the Father, "which," He said, "you have heard from Me."

Do you realize that a command is not a suggestion? A command means there is no option. He wanted them to do what He commanded.

It is obvious they did not already have that power He mentioned because if they had had it, they would not have had to receive it. But Jesus deemed that they needed it. And He told them not to leave Jerusalem until they received the Promise of the Father.

He told them they would receive the power after the Holy Spirit came upon them.

Some people will try to tell you that the Holy Spirit only had application for those original disciples. That could not be true because those people did not know about many of the places in the world. They would never get to go into the uttermost parts of the earth. It had to be talking to them, to whom those original ones would minister, and then that Word would be promulgated and finally it would cover the earth. It had to be talking about more than just those persons who were there physically at the time of Pentecost.

The Devil Hates Tongues

Acts 2 tells us that there were approximately 120 persons in the Upper Room and every one of them got filled with the Holy Spirit and began to speak with new tongues.

Now if you are a Believer, why don't you speak with new tongues? If your church does not preach and teach speaking with tongues, it is a dead church, and you have no right to put God's tithe there. They are not giving you the whole counsel of God.

If your church is speaking the whole counsel of God, then people will be speaking with other tongues — that is a sign that they are filled with the Holy Spirit. Whenever any kind of manifested sign is mentioned in reference to people being filled with the Holy Spirit, that sign is always speaking with other tongues.

Now why in the world are tongues so important and why does the devil fight them so much?

1 Corinthians 14:2:

For he who speaks in a tongue does not speak to men but to God, for no one understands him; however, in the spirit he speaks mysteries.

You can see why the devil would fight speaking in tongues. Because the devil cannot monitor what you are saying and he cannot interfere with it or influence it because you are talking to God. If he can scare you off from talking to God in tongues, then he can always know what you are saying. That way, he can get a jump on you and interfere with what you are saying. But when you are speaking in a language that he does not understand, you can close him out.

The term *mysteries* simply means mysteries as far as your human intellect is concerned, but you understand in the spirit.

Look at 1 Corinthians 14:4:

He who speaks in a tongue edifies himself...

That means you build yourself up. That is why Satan fights tongues. If you are not built up, then you will be weak. If you are weak, you are an easy pushover for him. He does not want you to build yourself up. You do not have to come to church to build yourself up. You can come to the church to hear the Word, to be instructed, to be taught, to be inspired, to be encouraged, to be directed. But you can build yourself up by praying or speaking with tongues. That is how you edify yourself. You do it for yourself. You build yourself up just like you do when you perform physical exercise.

Jude 20:

But you, beloved, building yourselves up on your most holy faith, praying in the Holy Spirit.

Now how do you pray in the Holy Spirit? By praying with other tongues. Praying with other tongues will not give you faith. You already have the faith. But you build yourself up on it by praying in the spirit, or praying with other tongues.

That is why Satan gets into pulpits and has preachers to delete speaking with tongues from the teaching of the Word of God. If the people do not know about tongues, they cannot participate in it. Satan can continue to monitor their prayers in English and then continue influencing them.

When you pray with other tongues, you don't know what you are saying so you cannot mess it up, and the devil doesn't know what you are saying so he cannot mess it up. Only your spirit knows what you are saying and God knows and interprets it. He gives it back to your spirit, your spirit instructs your mind, your mind directs your body and you are back in business. These are just a couple of controversial things, but they are not the purpose of this teaching of God's financial plan. Still, I want you to at least be aware of these important and very controversial issues.

If You Have Been Stealing — Pay Up!

There is a financial curse on people who rob God. When you steal the tithe and take what belongs to God, you are in a curse. It is hard to pay God back when you have been stealing.

I stopped stealing from God, and now instead of me owing God, He owes me. Did you know that God could owe you? He can. Even in reference to the poor. He said those who have pity on the poor lend to the Lord and He will repay it. God will repay when you give to the poor. It's in Proverbs 19:17.

Now if you want anybody to owe you, let the Lord owe you, because He pays his bills.

Do Not Pay Tithe to the Dead

When I found out that I had been robbing God, and there was no way that I could compute it because I had robbed Him for so many years, I decided on a way that I could straighten things out. It wasn't that God made me do it, because the Lord is merciful when you don't know. But He won't put up with any mess from you when you do know. You can fool one another, but you can't fool the Lord.

I wanted to be sure that I was on the plus side of the ledger, so I started tithing. I used the principle of percentage and started increasing my giving that I considered to be tithes over the years, because I knew I had robbed God. I don't feel that God would have made me give it back. I was not under compulsion to do it, but I wanted to because I was so grateful for finding out that I was robbing God and I did not have to rob Him anymore. I was thankful He did not cut me off, but was merciful, and that He allowed me to get to a point to receive the Word rather than follow the tradition of men.

Now 10 percent is all the tithe I have to pay in order to be a tither, but I started giving 12 percent, then 15 percent, then 20 percent, then 25 percent and now I give 30 percent of everything I get. I wanted to make up for what I thought I had robbed God of. I appreciated finally finding out the truth. When I think about what He has given to me and given for me through Christ, I really ought to give Him 90 percent and live on 10 percent. Now, I know I have more than paid it back. But it is so good; I just got habituated to it.

If somebody gives me $1,000, the first thing I think of is, *What is 30 percent of it?* My mind is trained to do that now. And thank God my wife is in agreement with it. It seems the more we give away, the more we receive. That is the law of sowing and reaping. It's beautiful because it helps you to be able to give to others and that is what is a blessing.

Let me show you the penalty that is built into the tithe. Look at Leviticus 27:30-31:

> **"And all of the tithe of the land, whether of the seed of the land or of the fruit of the tree, is the LORD'S. It is holy to the LORD.**
>
> **"If a man wants at all to redeem any of his tithes, he shall add one-fifth to it."**

The tithe is holy. When you steal the tithe, you are taking something that is holy for an unholy purpose.

Let's say your tithe is $10. If you take $5 out of your tithe, then you have robbed God of $5. So the next time you pay your tithes, instead of the 10 percent that you would normally pay, you have to pay $10 plus the $5 that you did not pay before, plus 20 percent of the $5 that you did pay. That's another dollar. So you would have to pay $16.

That sounds like nothing unless you are talking about thousands of dollars, but it can become expensive. It is to your advantage not to fall behind on your tithes.

Some of you robbed with knowledge. You are going to have to pay that 20 percent back. You may say you don't understand that and it sounds like bondage, but you put yourself under bondage by stealing from God.

Let me equate the principle with being overweight. Losing weight is not really the problem. Yes, it will be a challenge for some people, but losing the weight is not really hard to do once you make up your mind to do it. What's hard is keeping it off.

Maintaining the weight level that you want is when the challenge comes. The secret of losing and keeping it off is that you have to change your way of thinking about food and eating. If you do not, you will go right back up the scale again.

If you have been robbing God for years, it is like a fat person who has been out of control for years. The older you get, the more challenging it becomes. Those 50-year-old muscles don't do what they did when they were 20; I don't care what you tell them. Do not stop telling them, but you will find they do not respond like they did when you were 20 years old.

So you have lost the weight, but you haven't changed your attitude about food and about eating, and you creep right back and start eating out of control again. Likewise, if you are going to stay with tithing, you have to change your mind about money. Because this is what tithing is about. It is about money.

To help yourself with tithing you have to be inventive. I had to begin to think differently. If I had $100, I had to think to myself I really only have $90, and if I limit my spending to the $90, then I would never rob God. That $10 belongs to Him.

So it is not a temptation for me to overspend now. You could not pay me to take the Lord's money. Sometimes the devil will try to suggest to me, "You know if you only gave 10 percent instead of that 30 percent, think about how much money you would have left." Then right away I rebuke that thought in Jesus' name. And I tell the devil, "If you don't shut up, I will push it up to 35 percent!" Once I made up my mind to do it, I have not missed tithing in more than 33 years.

So don't obligate yourself for more than the $90 of every $100, and you will be all right.

When you rob God you hurt yourself; you hurt God only to the extent of what He will be able to do through you, because when your channel is jammed up, God is jammed up. When you rob God, it is like having a stroke in the sense that God cannot work through your body fully and freely like He wants to. When He attempts to walk you have this disabling condition that hinders Him from working through you. God is limited, just as you would be physically limited if your body parts were not all functioning correctly.

When you commit your life to Christ, your life includes everything — your devotion, your energy, your effort, your talent, your money, your time, His tithe.

Most of us are really playing catch-up in terms of the things of God. Now that you know about tithing, you are without excuse. Begin to operate now in what you know and experience the rewards of your obedience to His Word.

About the Author

Dr. Frederick K.C. Price is the founder and pastor of Crenshaw Christian Center in Los Angeles, California and Crenshaw Christian Center East in Manhattan, New York. He is known worldwide as a teacher of the biblical principles of faith, healing, prosperity and the Holy Spirit. During his more than 50 years in ministry, countless lives have been changed by his dynamic and insightful teachings that truly "tell it like it is."

His television program, *Ever Increasing Faith (EIF)*, has been broadcast throughout the world for more than 25 years and currently airs in 15 of the 20 largest markets in America, reaching an audience of more than 15 million households each week. EIF is also webcast on the Internet via www.faithdome.org. The EIF radio program is heard on stations across the world, including the continent of Europe via short-wave radio.

Author of more than 50 popular books teaching practical application of biblical principles, Dr. Price pastors one of America's largest church congregations, with a membership of approximately 22,000. The Los Angeles church sanctuary, the FaithDome, is among the most notable and largest in the nation, with seating capacity of more than 10,000.

In 1990, Dr. Price founded the Fellowship of Inner-City Word of Faith Ministries (FICWFM). Members of FICWFM include more than 300 churches from all over the United States and various countries. The Fellowship, which meets regionally throughout the year and hosts an annual convention, is not a denomination. Its mission is to provide fellowship, leadership, guidance and a spiritual covering for those desiring a standard of excellence in ministry. Members share methods and experiences commonly faced by ministries in the inner cities. Their focus is how to apply the Word of Faith to solve their challenges.

Dr. Price holds an honorary Doctorate of Divinity degree from Oral Roberts University and an honorary diploma from Rhema Bible Training Center.

On September 6, 2000, Dr. Price was the first black pastor to speak at Town Hall Los Angeles. He is the recipient of two prestigious awards. He is a 1998 recipient of the Horatio Alger Award. Each year, this prestigious honor is bestowed upon ten "outstanding Americans who exemplify inspirational success, triumph over adversity, and an uncommon commitment to helping others ...." He also received the 1998 Southern Christian Leadership Conference's Kelly Miller Smith Interfaith Award. This award is given to clergy who have made the most significant contribution through religious expression affecting the nation and the world.

Books by
Frederick K.C. Price, D.D.

WHY SHOULD CHRISTIANS SUFFER?

WORDS OF WISDOM: WOW!

EVER INCREASING FAITH STUDY JOURNAL
A Recorded Treasury of Personal Study Notes

GROWING IN GOD'S WORD:
Devotional & Prayer Journal

THE PURPOSE OF PROSPERITY

INTEGRITY
The Guarantee for Success

HIGHER FINANCE
How to Live Debt-Free

RACE, RELIGION & RACISM, VOLUME 1
A Bold Encounter With Division in the Church

RACE, RELIGION & RACISM, VOLUME 2
Perverting the Gospel to Subjugate a People

RACE, RELIGION & RACISM, VOLUME 3
Jesus, Christianity and Islam

THE TRUTH ABOUT ... THE BIBLE

THE TRUTH ABOUT ... DEATH

THE TRUTH ABOUT ... DISASTERS

THE TRUTH ABOUT ... FATE

THE TRUTH ABOUT ... FEAR

THE TRUTH ABOUT ... HOMOSEXUALITY

HIGHER FINANCE

THE TRUTH ABOUT . . . RACE

THE TRUTH ABOUT . . . WORRY

THE TRUTH ABOUT . . . GIVING

LIVING IN HOSTILE TERRITORY
A Survival Guide for the Overcoming Christian

DR. PRICE'S GOLDEN NUGGETS
A Treasury of Wisdom for Both Ministers and Laypeople

BUILDING ON A FIRM FOUNDATION

FIVE LITTLE FOXES OF FAITH

THE CHRISTIAN FAMILY:
Practical Insight for Family Living

IDENTIFIED WITH CHRIST:
A Complete Cycle From Defeat to Victory

THE CHASTENING OF THE LORD

TESTING THE SPIRITS

BEWARE! THE LIES OF SATAN

THE WAY, THE WALK,
AND THE WARFARE OF THE BELIEVER
(A Verse-by-Verse Study on the Book of Ephesians)

THREE KEYS TO POSITIVE CONFESSION

THE PROMISED LAND
(A New Era for the Body of Christ)

A NEW LAW FOR A NEW PEOPLE

THE VICTORIOUS, OVERCOMING LIFE
(A Verse-by-Verse Study on the Book of Colossians)

Books by Frederick K.C. Price, D.D.

NAME IT! AND CLAIM IT!
The Power of Positive Confession

*PRACTICAL SUGGESTIONS FOR
SUCCESSFUL MINISTRY*

WALKING IN GOD'S WORD
Through His Promises

THE HOLY SPIRIT:
The Helper We All Need

HOMOSEXUALITY:
State of Birth or State of Mind?

CONCERNING THOSE WHO HAVE FALLEN ASLEEP

THE ORIGIN OF SATAN

LIVING IN THE REALM OF THE SPIRIT

HOW TO BELIEVE GOD FOR A MATE

THANK GOD FOR EVERYTHING?

THE HOLY SPIRIT —
The Missing Ingredient

NOW FAITH IS

HOW TO OBTAIN STRONG FAITH
Six Principles

THE FAITHFULNESS OF GOD

IS HEALING FOR ALL?

HOW FAITH WORKS

FAITH'S GREATEST ENEMIES

To receive Dr. Price's book and tape catalog
or be placed on the EIF mailing list,
please call:

(800) 927-3436

*Books are also available
at local bookstores everywhere.*

For more information, please write:

**Crenshaw Christian Center
P.O. Box 90000
Los Angeles, CA 90009**

or check your local TV or Webcast listing:

Ever Increasing Faith Ministries

or visit our Website:

www.faithdome.org